LIFE IN GOD

LIFE IN GOD

Martyn Lloyd-Jones

LIFE IN CHRIST □ VOLUME FIVE

STUDIES IN 1 JOHN

CROSSWAY BOOKS

WHEATON, ILLINOIS • NOTTINGHAM, ENGLAND

CREDO

Life in God

Copyright © 1995 by Elizabeth Catherwood and Ann Desmond

First U.S. edition published 1994 by Crossway Books, a division of Good News Publishers, 1300 Crescent Street, Wheaton, Illinois 60187

Published in association with Credo Books, P.O. Box 3175, Langley, B.C., Canada V3A 4R5

Cover illustration: Keith Stubblefield

First printing, 1995

Printed in the United States of America

Library of Congress Cataloging-in-Publication Data
Lloyd-Jones, David Martyn.
    Life in God.
    Includes bibliographical references.
    Contents: v. 1. Fellowship with God—v. 2. Walking with God—
v. 3. Children of God—v. 4. The Love of God—v. 5. Life in God.
    1. Bible. N.T. Epistle of John, 1st—Sermons. 2. Sermons,
English. I. Title.
BS2805.4.L58 1995   227'.9406   95-21507
ISBN 0-89107-829-0

03		02		01		00										
15	14	13	12	11	10	9	8	7	6	5	4	3	2			

First British Edition 1994

ISBN 1-85684-092-1

Production and Printing in the United States of America for
CROSSWAY BOOKS
Norton Street, Nottingham, England NG7 3HR

TABLE OF CONTENTS

ACKNOWLEDGEMENTS

As usual, these sermons were edited by Christopher Catherwood, the Doctor's eldest grandson. But as with all the sermons published since the death of Dr. Lloyd-Jones in 1981, a major role was played by the Doctor's eldest daughter, Elizabeth Catherwood, who in her capacity as literary executrix went through all the editing to make sure that it was fully in accord with what the Doctor would have wanted had he been alive to supervise the work. Special thanks are therefore due to her for all her hard work, and also to Alison Walley for copy editing the manuscript and for putting it onto disk ready for the publisher.

1

The New Testament Definition of a Christian

Whosoever believeth that Jesus is the Christ is born of
God: and every one that loveth him that begat loveth him
also that is begotten of him.

1 JOHN 5:1

The Puritans had a very interesting phrase that they often
employed when they returned to a verse on which they
had already preached. Their way of putting it was that they
felt 'there were further gleanings that they could obtain from that
particular crop.' I think that is a very good way of referring to the
abundant lessons that are to be found so constantly in certain verses
we encounter in working through a section or portion of Scripture.

In our study of the previous chapter[1] we took this verse
together with the three concluding verses of chapter 4. Indeed, we
indicated that in these four verses together the Apostle is winding
up his great argument with regard to love for the brethren. And
there is no doubt at all that his main purpose in using the words we
have there was to provide a very powerful argument that is to be

deduced from the family relationship, in support of his contention that as Christians we should love one another.

That was his main reason, but, as I hinted, there is a great deal more in this verse than just that particular argument. And that leads me to make a statement that, I believe, is of great importance whenever we read the Bible. Invariably in Scripture there is not only the immediate argument, but there is also something further suggested. Or let me put it like this: observe the tremendous assumption that John makes in using this particular argument with these people, the basis on which his argument rests. Or, to put it another way, observe what he takes for granted in the understanding of these Christian people.

That is what I want to consider here. He is taking it for granted that they are perfectly familiar with the doctrine of regeneration and rebirth, and it is because he takes this for granted that he is able to draw that deduction. Thus, in arriving at that particular argument by referring to a family relationship, John, incidentally, is stating this profound doctrine of regeneration. This is characteristic of these New Testament Apostles; they assume the acceptance of certain fundamental doctrines on the part of the people, so that there is a sense in which we can say that we simply cannot follow their detailed argument unless we start by accepting the basic doctrine on which everything is founded. So once more we find John apparently repeating himself. He has already dealt with this idea of being born again, being born of God, several times, and yet he returns to it. But in actual practise he is not repeating himself; he always has some particular shade of meaning, something fresh to present, some new aspect of the matter, and as we look at this verse we shall find that he is doing so once more.

Or we can look at this in another way and say that we have here, once again, one of those synopses of Christian doctrine that are such a characteristic feature of this Apostle. John was very fond of stating the whole of the Christian faith in a verse, and this is not only characteristic of John but of the entire New Testament. The

Apostle Paul did the same thing; these men realised that nothing was more important than that the people to whom they wrote, and therefore Christians at all times, should always be grasping the entire Christian truth. There is no meaning, no sense in particular arguments unless they are derived from the whole body of doctrine.

I emphasise all this because I believe increasingly that the main difficulty with many people today is that they are so interested in particular matters that they fail to connect them with this whole corpus of doctrine. As a result, they find themselves in trouble and in perplexity. So if we would know something about the relationship of the Christian to politics and worldly affairs, for example, the only way to do so is not to start with a particular question, but to start with the whole truth and then to draw our deduction.

Therefore the Apostle, in elaborating the argument about brotherly love, incidentally reminds us of the whole truth. Now this subject can be best divided into two main sections, since John makes two main statements. The first is this: what makes us Christian is the rebirth; we must be born again. John more or less assumes this. He says, 'Whosoever believeth that Jesus is the Christ is born of God: and every one that loveth him that begat loveth him also that is begotten of him.' 'Now,' says John in effect, 'I am anxious to demonstrate to you this question of the importance of loving the brethren; and, of course, it follows quite inevitably from the doctrine of the rebirth that you know all about.'

However, as I have already suggested, we live in an age when we cannot make any such assumptions, so that we have to lay this down as a proposition. Indeed, as we read words like these, must not we plead guilty in general to the charge that our ideas of the Christian position are totally inadequate and insufficient; must we not admit our failure? Indeed, I believe that most of the difficulties in this connection tend to arise from the fact that we will persist in thinking of it in terms of something that we are, our faith, our belief, our action, our good works, instead of thinking of it in the way in which the New Testament itself puts it.

To test what I am trying to convey, let us ask ourselves some questions. What is my conception of the Christian? What is it that makes one a Christian at all? Upon what do I base my claim of being a Christian? If I am asked by somebody, 'You call yourself a Christian—what are your reasons for doing so?' what would be my reply? Now, I am afraid that far too often we would find that our answers fall very far short of the statement that we have here in this verse, the verse that I want to show you is typical of the whole of the New Testament teaching.

The first thing we must get rid of is this idea that what makes us Christian is anything that we have produced or anything for which we are responsible. The New Testament at once shows us the total inadequacy of the common, current version of what constitutes a Christian. The New Testament terms are *regeneration*, *a new creation*, being *born again*. Those are its categories, and it is only as we stand face to face with them that we begin to realise what a tremendous thing it is to be a Christian. But let me analyse that a little in the terms John uses here. The first thing, therefore, is that what makes men and women Christians is something that is done to them by God, not something they do themselves—'Whosoever believeth that Jesus is the Christ is born of God.' And then, 'Every one that loveth him that begat.' God, according to John, is the one who begets us; it is God's action, not ours.

Now we need not take time in emphasising the obvious contrast in each of these subdivisions. How ready we are to think of being a Christian as the result of something that we do! I live a good life, therefore I am a Christian; I go to a place of worship, therefore I am a Christian; I do not do certain things, therefore I am a Christian; I believe, therefore I am a Christian. The whole emphasis is upon myself, upon what I do. Whereas here, at the very beginning of the New Testament definition of a Christian, the entire emphasis is not upon man and his activity, but upon God. *He* who begat, *He* who produced, *He* who generates, *He* who gives life and being. Thus we see that we cannot be a Christian at all unless God has done something to us.

But I go beyond that and say in the second place that what makes us a Christian is something that makes us like God. 'Whosoever believeth that Jesus is the Christ is born of God.' That '*of*' is an important word; it means 'out of God'; this is one who has received something of God Himself. Therefore, the action of God in making us Christian is not merely an external one; it does not merely touch us on the outside. And in this respect we must always be very careful in our use of the word 'creation.' When God created the world He did not impart Himself to it—He made it outside Himself. But in the new creation, in the rebirth that makes us Christian, the New Testament teaching is that we do receive something of God's own nature. We have been made 'partakers,' says Peter, 'of the divine nature' (2 Pet 1:4); we are sharers in and participators of it. So the New Testament idea of what makes us Christian is not that we happen to be born in a certain country, nor that our parents happen to be Christians. Not at all! Rather, it is nothing less than that we have been born out of God; we are those who have received something of the divine nature.

Now we have to be very careful with this doctrine; we must not think of it in any material sense. It does not mean that I receive some kind of essence or something tangible and material. But it does mean that I receive the spiritual nature and the spiritual outlook and disposition of God Himself. To be born again means to receive this new disposition; that is what is meant by 'a new nature.' So it is something that is done to us by God that makes us like God. Therefore, I go on to deduce that it is something that makes an essential difference *to* us and something that also makes an essential difference *in* us.

In other words, according to the New Testament, when we become Christian we are entirely unlike what we were before. 'If any man be in Christ,' says Paul, 'he is a new creature: old things are passed away; behold, all things are become new' (2 Cor 5:17).

I am transformed—profound language for the change that takes place when a person becomes a Christian. I am showing you how utterly superficial the current notions are; because it is the action of God upon us, it is as profound as that. I am, yet not I; I am something essentially different, and indeed I must be if I have now become a partaker of the divine nature. Therefore, when men and women become Christians they are aware of this great difference in their lives. They can contrast their present self with their former self. Now I am not insisting upon their being able to point to a particular moment. All I am saying is that those who are Christians realise there is that about their lives that was not once the case. There is an awareness of this divine action; they are different from what they once were.

I would also put it like this, that Christians are always aware of the fact that they are essentially different from those who are not Christians. Now the moment one says a thing like that, the response of the men of the world is: 'That is typical of you Christians; it is your spiritual pride. You say, "I thank God I am not like other people."' Well, yes, if I am a Christian at all I must say that; but the way in which I do so is of tremendous importance. The Pharisee said it in that way: 'God, I thank thee, that I am not as other men are.' He was proud of himself, and he despised the publican (Luke 18:9-15).

Christians do not say it like that, but rather with profound humility. They say, 'I thank God that I am not as that other poor man still is and as I once was. I thank God that He has not left me in that state and condition, that He has acted upon me and given me a new birth.' They are not priding themselves. Their pride is in God, in Christ's activity within them. So we must not be guilty of this false and spurious modesty. If I am not thankful to God that I am not like the worldling who is living in sin and vice, I am not a Christian at all. I should rejoice in the fact that God has had mercy upon me and has dealt with me and has made me so different from the men and women of the world who do not know Him and do not see their need of Christ. It follows of necessity that if we are born of God, we must obviously be very different from those who are not, and we should rejoice in the difference. So the last deduction is that this activity of God upon us is something that makes us like all other Christians. 'Whosoever believeth that Jesus is the Christ is born of God: and every one that loveth him that begat loveth him also that is begotten of him.' All those who are begotten of Him must be alike, because they are all begotten of Him. So, you see, it is a simple deduction. As a Christian I am new and different from what I once was; I am different from the person who is not a Christian. But of necessity I must be like all who are Christians. There is a likeness in the members of a family; those who are begotten of the same father have the marks and the traces of the common parenthood upon them. In the same way, there is a likeness about the people of God, and this is one of the most glorious things about being a Christian. You recognise the others, you see the likeness in them; it is a very good test of whether we are Christians at all that we can recognise a brother or sister. We see the mark, and we understand it.

Now that is where, I think, we have one of those final proofs that being a Christian means to be born again. For by natural birth and temperament we are all so very different; as we were by nature, we would not recognise an affinity with those whom we may heartily dislike and with whom we have nothing in common. But the essential thing about the Christian position is that we recognise something in common with people who by nature and birth are different. So the Church is thus in herself a standing testimony of the doctrine of rebirth. In the Christian Church you have people of every conceivable temperament and psychological makeup, and yet they are all one. Why? Because they recognise this common element. They have all been begotten of the same Father, and they love one another because they recognise this similarity and likeness, this common inheritance that they share together.

There, then, are some of the deductions that we draw from this profound New Testament concept as to what it is that makes us

Christians—born of God, begotten of God. Therefore, I ask the obvious question at this point: are we aware of the fact that God has begotten us? Do we know that God has produced a man or woman in us that is not ourselves and not of ourselves? As we examine ourselves have we come to say, 'I am what I am by the grace of God. Not by my activities, nor by my interest; not by my belief, nor by the fact that I do or do not do certain things. I am what I am by the grace of God who has brought me to a rebirth and who has given me His own nature and disposition'?

John assumes that; it is the New Testament assumption everywhere about the Christian. Again I must say it—what a tremendous thing it is to be a Christian! Oh, how we vie with one another in seeking earthly honours; how we try to prove that we are related, however remotely, to somebody who happens to be great—we attach great importance to these things. Yet what the humblest Christian can claim is that he is a child of God, born of God, out of God, generated by God; that is the very essence of what is meant, according to the New Testament, by being a Christian.

The second great principle is the results, or the fruits, of the rebirth. How may we know that we are Christians in this sense? What is the first fruit of being born again? Well, according to John, it is faith, *belief*. Here, again, is a very important and interesting matter. 'Whosoever *believeth* that Jesus is the Christ is born of God.' You can see that He is essential. 'Show me someone,' says John, 'who believes that Jesus is the Christ, and I say there is a person who has been born of God.' John means this. There is no such thing as believing or having faith, in a Christian sense, without the rebirth. Now, all who are in any sense interested in theology must be interested in that question: which comes first—belief or being born again? Well, according to John here, and I think I can show you that it is the same everywhere in the New Testament, it is the rebirth that comes first, and then faith. The first expression of being born again is that one believes.

Let me put it to you like this: our estate by nature, according to the New Testament, is that we are dead in trespasses and in sin. Are the dead capable of any action; can a dead man believe? Surely before you believe you must be alive, and you cannot be alive without being born. Take the way in which the Apostle Paul works it out very plainly and explicitly: 'The natural man receiveth not the things of the Spirit of God: for they are foolishness unto him: neither can he . . .' (1 Cor 2:14). 'But you and I,' says Paul in effect, 'we believe these things.' Why? Because we have received the Spirit, the Spirit who is not of this world, the Spirit who is of God, and 'the Spirit searcheth all things, yea, the deep things of God' (1 Cor 2:10). Indeed, we have received this Spirit 'that we might know the things that are freely given to us of God' (v. 12).

There is a great tragedy before us, says the Apostle to the Corinthians. The very Lord of glory, the Lord Jesus Christ, came into this world, and He stood before men. He spoke to them; He worked miracles in their presence; but the very 'princes' of the world did not believe in Him. They were men of ability; there is no doubt but that 'princes' would refer not only to royal blood, but philosophers, men who are princes in every natural sense. They did not believe on Him. And the reason for this? Because they had not received the Spirit of God; no one can say that Jesus is the Lord but by the Holy Spirit. There is no such thing as faith or belief without rebirth. 'Whosoever believeth that Jesus is the Christ is born of God'; he must be born again—he cannot believe without the new birth. There is nothing, in a sense, that seems to be so contrary to the New Testament teaching as the suggestion that as a natural man I believe and because I believe, I am given the rebirth. The dead cannot believe; the natural man cannot. He is at enmity against God; he is incapable of this. The very fact that a man believes is proof he has been born again; it is the first fruit that is manifested in the life of one who has been born of God.

But let me emphasise also *what* he believes. 'Whosoever believeth that *Jesus is the Christ* is born of God.' Here again is something of great importance to us. Men and women who are

Christians are people who have been born again, and the first proof
they give that this has happened is that they believe that 'Jesus is
the Christ.' You see, John never separates doctrine and experience;
they always go together. Christians not only believe in the being
and existence of God. There are large numbers of people in the
world who believe in God who are not Christians. To believe in
God and in the holiness of God and many other things about Him
does not make one a Christian. Christian faith is a specific belief—
that 'Jesus is the Christ.' In other words, our whole faith must be
focused on the Lord Jesus Christ; it is what we believe about Him
that makes us Christian.

We must believe that Jesus of Nazareth, that person who
belongs to history, that man who worked as a carpenter for all those
years and went about preaching and healing, we must believe that
He is the Christ, the Messiah, the anointed of God. By this John
means that it is in Christ and through Christ alone that salvation is
possible to us. The Messiah is the one who is appointed by God to
deliver His people. Now, the Jews thought of that in a material,
political sense, and because our Lord did not prepare a great army
and did not go to Jerusalem to be crowned as King, they said He
was not the Messiah. But the whole teaching of the New Testament
is to show that He *is* the Messiah, the promised deliverer, a spiritual
deliverer. Thus to believe that 'Jesus is the Christ' really means that
we say and believe there is no salvation at all possible for us apart
from Him.

That is the very essence of the New Testament teaching; yet I
am increasingly amazed at the failure of people to understand it. I
put this question to people very frequently. I say, 'If you had to die
tonight, on what would you rely in the presence of God? What
would you say to Him?' And they tell me, 'Well, I would ask Him
to forgive me—I believe He is ready to pardon,' and they go on talking, but they never mention the name of the Lord Jesus Christ.

But to be in that position is not to be a Christian at all. The first
thing the Christian believes is that 'Jesus is the Christ.' It is to

believe, therefore, that He is the Son of God in a unique sense, that He is the eternal Son of God made flesh, that He bore our sins in his own body on the tree (1 Pet 2:24), and that it is only because our sins were punished in Him that God forgives us. It is in that way that He delivers us and sets us free. He rose again to justify us; He is seated at the right hand of God, waiting until His enemies shall be made His footstool. He will return again and destroy evil from the face of the earth and introduce His glorious Kingdom—'Jesus is the Christ.'

Thus the first fruit of the rebirth is that I believe that. And obviously, believing that is not something intellectual or something I only do with my mind. If I believe, I commit my whole life to Him. If I believe, I know I am delivered because Christ has done that for me. I see that apart from Him I am lost and undone and doomed. This is a profound action; it is a commitment; it is a banking of one's everything upon that fact.

The second fruit of the rebirth is *love for God.* John's way of putting it is: 'every one that loveth him that begat . . .' Christians see that they are hell-deserving sinners and that they would have arrived in hell were it not for His great love in sending His Son. They realise the love of God for them, and therefore they love God; they realise they owe everything to Him. It seems to me that this again is one of those fundamental things about Christian men and women. However good a life they may be living now as saints, they still feel that they are hell-deserving sinners in and of themselves, and that they owe everything to the grace of God; that it is God's love alone that has made them what they are. They lose their sense of fear and a sense of enmity against God and are filled with a sense of profound gratitude to Him.

Do we know this gratitude? You see, if we are relying upon ourselves and our good life and our actions and our beliefs, we do not feel much gratitude to God because we have done it all ourselves, and we are grateful to ourselves for being what we are. But if we realise that we are nothing and that God has given us everything, then we shall feel this gratitude; we shall love Him who has begotten us.

And the final thing is, of course, that we *love our brethren*– 'Every one that loveth him that begat loveth him also that is begotten of him.' This needs no demonstration. We look at those others, and we see in them the same disposition as in ourselves. We realise that they owe everything to the grace of God, just as we do. We realise that in spite of their sinfulness God sent His Son to die for them, exactly as He did for us; and we are aware of this bond. Though there may be many things about them we do not like, we say, 'That is my brother, my sister.' So we begin to love them, and we are marching together to that land that God has prepared for us.

There, then, we have the fruits, the results, of rebirth–faith and belief; love for God who has begotten us; and love for those who are, like ourselves, begotten of God by His wondrous grace.

That is the New Testament idea of a Christian. How tawdry do worldly honours and ideas seem to be in the light of this; the things for which people vie and compete, the things about which they get so excited, these glittering prizes after which they run; oh, how small, how unworthy! But we are born of God; we are children of God, heirs of God, joint heirs with Christ. We belong to the royal family of heaven, to the King of kings and Lord of lords, and we are partakers of His divine nature. Let us rise and be worthy of the high calling of God in Christ Jesus our Lord.

2

The Wholeness of the Christian Life

By this we know that we love the children of God, when we love God, and keep his commandments. For this is the love of God, that we keep his commandments: and his commandments are not grievous.

1 JOHN 5:2-3

In these two verses we come to one of those places of transition in the movement of the thought of the Apostle. Consequently, these two verses are really of very great significance in an understanding of the argument that is being evolved by the writer. Our analysis of the epistle, let me remind you,[1] is to tell Christian people that even in a world like this a fulness of joy is possible. The Apostle when he wrote this letter had become an old man; he was facing the end of his life, and he wanted to leave this word of comfort and encouragement with these first Christians, and this is his message. It is a very realistic message; he paints no rosy picture of a world that is going to get better and better until everything is going to be perfect. Rather, he puts it in its stark nakedness; it is a world that 'lieth in the evil one.' Yet in spite of that—and this is the essential message of the gospel—there is a joy that, as Peter says, is

21

'unspeakable and full of glory' (1 Pet 1:8). And John says that this is possible because we can, in this world and even as we are, have fellowship with God; it is fellowship with God that leads to joy.

Then we have been indicating that John, as a wise pastor and teacher, has been warning these people that there are certain things that will rob them of that joy unless they are careful. God's promises are always conditional, and here John tells us that there are very definite conditions that we must observe. You can look at this either negatively or positively; there are things we must avoid, and there are things we have to observe, and here are the three main things that he keeps on emphasising. Firstly, if we want to enjoy that fellowship with God, we must keep His commandments; secondly, if we want to enjoy that fellowship, we must love the brethren—love one another; and, thirdly, we must always be right in our doctrine, and especially the doctrine concerning the absolute centrality and necessity of the Lord Jesus Christ.

Now John constantly illustrates these things, and he puts it in two main ways like this: Firstly, we must always realise in this world that we can have that fellowship with God; and, secondly, we must realise that we are children of God. I have shown that by the end of the sixth verse of the fourth chapter the Apostle has worked out those two main lines. In a sense he has finished his argument at that point, and from there on, I have suggested,[2] he just takes up these major themes again and elaborates them. He was anxious that these people should enjoy the benefits. So, having stated the case, he says, 'now let me sum it up; these are the things you have to watch,' and this is the order in which he puts them: love for the brethren; keeping the commandments; and unswerving loyalty and adherence to the message and the faith concerning the Lord Jesus Christ. And he elaborates these three themes.

We have considered the theme of brotherly love that starts in chapter 4, verse 7,[3] and we finished in the last study [of *The Love of God*] at the end of the first verse in chapter 5. Now, in verses 2 and 3, we come to the point of transition. John is talking about another of his themes, and the way in which he does so is most interesting. John's style sometimes seems to be rather difficult. There is a sense in which he is very much more difficult than the Apostle Paul, and for this reason: the difference between the two writers is that the Apostle Paul always tells you what he is doing before he does it; but John does it without telling you and, as it were, leaves you to find out what he is doing! I suppose in many ways it is the difference between the man who is centrally and primarily logical and who reasons, and the man who is more musical. John's characteristic method is that when he is making a transition from one theme to another, he does not put a full stop and say, 'Now let us look at so and so'—not a bit! Rather he glides from one to another. I believe that perhaps the best way of putting it is to use this musical illustration: you often find in a symphony or something like that, where there are a number of themes, that the composer very often, just as he is finishing one theme, throws out a hint of the one that is coming. Indeed he may do that some time before he really takes up the second theme.

Now that is what John does here. He has been dealing with the theme of love for the brethren, and he says, 'By this we know that we love the children of God'—you can see he is still on the theme of love for the brethren, but he hasn't yet finished the subject—'by this we know that we love the children of God, when we love God, and keep his commandments.' There is a hint of the theme that is coming, and then he takes up that theme: 'For this is the love of God, that we keep his commandments: and his commandments are not grievous. For whatsoever is born of God overcometh the world'; there is the hint of the next theme. That is his method—this gliding from one to the other.

This is a very important point because it really does remind us in a very forcible and striking manner of the whole theme of this first Epistle of John. It is, in a sense, life, life in God, life and its manifestations, so that in many ways there is a great deal to be said for John and for his method. John did not regard the Christian faith so much as a series of propositions; to him it was essentially a matter of life. Now putting it like that may give the impression that Paul did not believe the Christian faith was life, and of course he did. But Paul was speaking of life in terms of his grand propositions, and John never really does that, because his main interest in life is that it is something vital and organic. It is something, in a sense, that you cannot analyse, something that manifests and shows itself and reveals itself in various ways.

So we can very readily say that the theme of his first epistle is this: the life that is given to man by God and the way in which it shows itself, and therefore the importance of examining ourselves to make sure we really have it. That is what he keeps on doing. 'You must test yourself,' he says; 'there are antichrists, false teachers; there is the devil who is suggesting things to you, so you always have to make quite sure–Beloved, believe not every spirit, but try the spirits whether they are of God; because many false prophets are gone out into the world' (4:1). So there it is–life and its manifestations and the importance of making sure we really have it. That is exactly what John does in this interesting way in which he moves from one theme to the other in these two verses; he presents us with the whole philosophy of his method and shows what he is really anxious to impress upon us.

Therefore, bearing all that in mind, let us come a little closer to these verses that are of such vital importance in a true understanding of the whole thesis. Let me put it to you like this: at first sight, when you read this second verse you may very well come to the conclusion that John is contradicting something that he has just been saying. He says, 'By this we know that we love the children of God, when we love God, and keep his commandments.' Surely, says someone, that is the opposite of what he said in 4:20–'If a man say, I love God, and hateth his brother, he is a liar: for he that loveth not his brother whom he hath seen, how can he love God whom he hath not seen?' The way, says John in that verse, in which you may know for certain that you love God is that you love your brother; and yet here he says that the way in which you make certain that you love your brother is that you love God! He is contradicting himself, some would charge.

However, there is no contradiction whatsoever in these two statements. John says that it is all entirely due to the fact that we are concerned with life; it is not a question of starting with one and advancing on to the other, but rather that if you have one you must have the other. I pointed out[4] in dealing with 4:20 that John was not saying you start by loving your brother and thereby come to love God—not at all! He says that these two things always go together.

Let me put all this in the form of a number of propositions. The first thing I find is what we may very well call 'the wholeness of the Christian life.' Life is always something vital and organic. The human body is not a collection of parts, of fingers and arms and forearms all somehow or another attached together. That is not the body at all. The body is organic—vital and essentially whole, and these are but parts of it. Thus in any analysis that we may make, and we must make one, we must always make it in terms of the whole. Take a flower; you can divide it up into petals and stamens and various other parts. But in making your analysis—if you want to do it properly—you must not pull out the petals and the stamens, because if you do you will have no flower at the end. You make your analysis, but you do not destroy anything.

It is exactly the same with life in every realm and department, and it is particularly true of this Christian life with which we are concerned and that John is expounding to us. You cannot understand this epistle without always holding in the centre of your mind the idea that the Christian life is a whole life. What God gives us is *life*. It is not that I believe certain things and do no more; God gives me life, and life manifests itself in certain ways. Furthermore, there are certain things that are absolute essentials to the Christian life, and John's case is that they must all be present in some shape or form before there is such a thing as the Christian life. Or, to put it negatively, the absence of any one of these elements should lead me, at any rate, to doubt very seriously whether there is life at all. Not only must all these things be present—they must all be present at the same time; and if any one of them is not there, then I must examine myself very seriously and query whether any of them is there.

Now this, I think you will see, is really a very important principle. Wherever there is life, certain things will always be there; there will be activity, there will be breathing, and so on. Where there is no breathing or some sort of activity, there is no life; and where there is no development there is no life. There are certain things that are essential before it can be said that a person is alive, and it is exactly like that in the spiritual life. John has already told us what these things are—love for God, keeping His commandments, loving the brethren, holding the faith; and John's argument is that all these are parts of the manifestation of the Christian life.

So we must not think of the Christian life merely as a matter of some external experience of God and certain feelings that I may have. I must not think of it either as merely living a certain type of ethical life or having certain feelings and sensations with regard to other people. Nor must I think of it in terms of holding certain intellectual propositions in my mind with regard to the Christian faith. Rather, the Christian life is a whole life, and there are certain elements that must always be present.

That is the first great proposition, and the second is that the way to test each or any part, therefore, is not so much to concentrate on that particular thing itself, but rather to look for the manifestation of the others. There, I think, we do come to the key to understanding John's particular method. Here I am looking at life, which is a whole thing, complete, organic; and now I want to examine one particular part. I may feel a certain amount of trouble in my mind with regard to one of these manifestations—is it really present in my life? Well, the best way to discover that, says John, is not so much to start with that particular thing, but to look and see if the other things are there. For if they are not, you have no life, and what you think is a manifestation of life is not that at all. And, John suggests, it does not matter much with which of these particular elements you start.

I like to think of this as a kind of circular movement. It does not matter really at which point you start in this circle. If you start at one point, you are bound to go on; and as you go around the circle, you pass these four points. You can think of it in terms of a clock. You set your clock going at the hour or the quarter or the half or the three-quarters, and if your clock is working you will duly pass the quarter and the half and the three quarters until you reach the hour, so that in reality it does not matter where you start.

Now that is the very principle on which John has been working. He sometimes starts with the love of God and goes on to the love of the brethren. At other times he starts with the love of the brethren and arrives at the love of God. And sometimes he starts with the commandments and then goes on to the love of the brethren and the love of God. It is immaterial. Here is a circle, and there are these particular points on it. Now because it is a circle, you must have the four points. If you do not have one, you do not have any; it is no longer a circle. You can start at whatever point you like, and if you want to know whether you are right on that point, make sure the others are also present.

In other words, the great thing to know is that we are on the circle, that we have the life; and we know that if we have life, it will manifest itself in certain ways. If I have one, I must have all; if I am doubtful of one, let me examine the rest. So at one time John says, 'If a man say, I love God, and hateth his brother, he is a liar'; he is testing there my love to God and takes me to the love of the brethren. And here, you see, it is a different method: 'By this we know that we love the children of God, when we love God, and keep his commandments.' So this concept of the Christian life as a whole, as an organic, vital, life-giving, living thing, is really of great importance when we come to this question of self-examination and concern about the parts; and that leads me to my next proposition.

'Why is this testing so important?' says someone. 'Why does
John keep on like this? Why didn't he finish his letter at chapter 4,
verse 6? Why go on repeating it?' He does it for one reason only,
which is that there is a horrible danger of the counterfeit. He has
constantly reminded us of that—the antichrists, the false teachers.
How easy it is to persuade ourselves that we have life when we do
not. How easy to say that the whole of the Christian life is just a
mystical feeling, or that it is just an attitude towards other people,
being nice and kind and friendly. How easy to say that the whole
of Christianity is just a certain moral quality of life and living, or
that what makes us Christian is reading books on theology and discussing them, and nothing else.

'No!' says John; 'the devil would have you do that. He would
focus your attention on something that appeals to you. I want you
to see,' he says, 'that if you do not have this wholeness, this fulness,
you are being deluded. You are being misled; the false teachers and
antichrists have led you astray.' This life is something that is whole.
If you have not got it all, you have not got any. It is not that you
have reached maturity when you start; a baby is perfect, and in that
newborn baby there is all the promise of the ultimate adult perfection. You can examine life almost in embryo, and it is as whole in
the embryo as it is in the fully matured adult.

Testing, therefore, is a very vital and urgent matter because of
this terrible possibility of self-delusion, and, of course, the importance of that arises in this way: if I do want to enjoy this fulness of
joy that John speaks of, if I want to know fellowship with God and
that I am a child of God, then I must be absolutely right about these
things. So if you lack assurance of salvation, if you are uncertain as
to whether you are a child of God, if you cannot say, 'Yes, I know
God, and I have fellowship with God, and I walk with God,' if you
are not in that position, I suggest that you have never done what
John is pressing upon us in this epistle. We must view it in this way
and be certain that we have it. Self-examination is not important
theoretically but from this essentially practical standpoint.

The last proposition is simply the working out of the mechanical process of testing, and John does it for us in these two verses. 'Let us start,' he says, 'with this question of loving the brethren. By this we know that we love the children of God . . .' In other words, I must be quite sure that I am really loving the brethren. I may have considered other parts of John's epistle and said, 'That is comforting and consoling. John seems to say that if I love the brethren, then I have the love of God.' But do I love the brethren? 'Well, make sure of it,' says John. There is such a thing as confusing a true Christian love for the brethren with just a liking.

We are all born very differently. Some people are born nice people, some are not. Some people are born with such an easy, almost phlegmatic nature and temperament that they can like almost anybody. They seem to like Christian people; they seem to like being in Christian society. They do not like the noise and bustle of the world. But they are not Christians; they are just born with that temperament. They rather like the atmosphere and society of the Church; they like mixing with people who are quiet. They like singing hymns, they try to live a good life, and they like the whole atmosphere of a place of worship. Such people have to be very careful, when they say they love the brethren, to make sure they are not just manifesting a natural liking. There are some people who instinctively like discussing Christian things. They have always been like that, and they may be right on the vitals of the Christian faith. 'Now there,' says John, 'you must examine yourself.'

And the way to test that is not just to analyse your own feelings and dissect them. Rather, this is the way to do it: 'By this we know that we love the children of God, when we love God.' So if I do not love God, what I have hitherto regarded as love for the brethren is not that at all, but simply this natural liking. In other words, as I go around the circle, can I say, 'I love God'? Because if I truly love Him, then I must be loving the brethren also—it is a part of the circle. So I must be quite sure that my love for the brethren is based upon the love of God and a love for God. I must be able to say quite honestly, 'I like these people not in a natural sense, but because I see in them the grace of God. Love for the brethren means love for the Christian brother or sister, so that what makes me love these people is the grace of the Lord Jesus Christ, the love of God in them, and the love of God working upon them; the thing that is in me I see in them. I am thereby very sure that it is not something elemental, but something that results from having received the life of God into my own soul.'

That is the first test, but it is not enough, because you might say to me, 'You seem to have solved one problem, but you have left me with another. You say I test my love of the brethren by saying, "Do I love God?" and yet some time ago you were telling me the only way to know God is to love the brethren.' 'Wait a minute,' says John, 'I haven't finished—by this we know that we love the children of God, when we love God, and keep his commandments.' So my immediate problem is this: at this point I am halfway around the face of the clock—do I love God? How can I know whether I love God? Once more John says, 'Don't just sit down and examine your mood and feelings; go on around the circle—when we love God, and keep his commandments.'

Here again, as I think we all must agree, there is nothing about which we can so deceive ourselves as about the fact that we love God. A man may come to me and say he loves God. He says with Browning, 'God's in His heaven,/All's right with the world'; but when something goes against him, he finds he does not love God. He says, 'Why does God . . . ?' Feelings are very deceptive. How do I know I love God? There is the next step—'*when we keep . . . his commandments.*'

Our Lord emphasises that in John 14:21: 'He that hath my commandments, and keepeth them, he it is that loveth me.' You cannot separate these things. Love is not a sentiment; it is the most active, vital thing in the world. If I love, I want to please—I keep the commandments; and what I may regard as the love of God in my

soul is a pure delusion unless it leads me to keep God's commandments and to live life as He wants me to live it.

'Again,' says someone, 'you have just shifted the problem; you
have got rid of two difficulties, but you have left me with the third.
This keeping of the commandments—what is this?' 'Well,' says John
in a kind of footnote on which he is going to elaborate in the next
verse, 'his commandments are not grievous'—not heavy. In other
words, what matters in this whole question of keeping the commandments is my attitude towards them. When I face the commandments of God, do I resent them? Do I feel that God is
imposing an impossible load upon me? Do I groan and grumble
and say, 'Oh, this hard taskmaster who asks of me the impossible!'?

'If that is your attitude towards the commandments of God,'
says John, 'you are not keeping them, and neither are you loving
God, and you are not loving your brethren—you are outside the life
altogether.' For someone who is truly Christian does not find the
commandments of God to go against the grain. He may be acutely
aware of his failure—if he is facing them truly he must be—but he
does not resent them, he loves them. He knows they are right, and
he wants to keep them and to love them. He does not feel they are
a heavy load imposed upon him; he says rather, 'This is right; that
is how I would like to live. I want to be like Christ Himself—His
commandments are not grievous.'

So here is a very thorough and practical test: is my Christian
living a task? Is it something that I resent and object to? Do I spend
my time trying to get out of it? Am I trying to compromise with the
life of the world? Am I just living on the edge of the Christian life,
or do I want to get right into the centre and live the life of God and
be perfect even as my Father in heaven is perfect? 'His commandments are not grievous' to Christian men and women; they know
that is what God asks of them. They love God and therefore they
want to keep His commandments.

There, then, it seems to me, are the practical tests as John works
them out for us. But let us always remember where we begin; it is

the wholeness that matters: loving God, keeping His commandments, loving the brethren, holding the faith.

Thank God for such a life; thank God for its wholeness, its fulness, its completeness, its balance, its perfection of form. Thank
God for this perfect thing that He gives us; and as we examine ourselves, let us never forget that the proof of life is that all the parts
are always present and always present together.

3

Overcomers

For whatsoever is born of God overcometh the world: and this is the victory that overcometh the world, even our faith. Who is he that overcometh the world, but he that believeth that Jesus is the Son of God?

1 JOHN 5:4-5

It is obvious from this word *For* at the beginning of the fourth verse that the Apostle here is continuing something that he has already mentioned; so in order to understand the statement of these two verses, we must remind ourselves of the previous verses. John has just been making the point that to the Christian the commandments of God are 'not grievous.' The way in which we show that we love God is that we keep His commands, and thus if we love God the commandments of necessity cannot be grievous; our very love of Him makes us desire to keep them.

'But that is not all,' says John, 'that is not enough.' John was anxious to help these people, so he does not leave it like that as a general statement; he elaborates it, and he takes it up by using this word *for*. 'By this we know that we love the children of God, when we love God, and keep his commandments. For this is the love of God, that we keep his commandments: and his commandments are not grievous. For [because] whatsoever is born of God overcometh the world.' That is why the commandments are not heavy; that is the connecting link.

Now that is the way in which John here, in these few verses, introduces us to this whole question—indeed, I may say this whole problem—of keeping the commandments of God. It is a problem because it is something at which Christian people very often stumble. The relationship of the Christian to the commandments of God has often been a point of great debate and dispute. There have been those who have emphasised the keeping of the commandments, who have more or less kept them to the letter and, in so pressing the commandments, have become legalistic. It is possible for Christians to become legalistic in their outlook, and they may put themselves under bondage. This had arisen in the early church, and that is why Paul, especially, had to write certain epistles, such as the Epistle to the Galatians, and probably also the one to the Romans. This also seems to be the background to the Epistle to the Hebrews. You find this sometimes put in this way, that people tend to see the end of the ceremonial law as the result of the work of grace, and yet say that the moral law still abides and obtains.

The second danger is what you might call the danger of *antinomianism*, and it has led many Christians into grievous error not only intellectually but often in life and vigour. They say, 'I am free from the law. Because I am now a Christian, I am no longer under the law but under grace, and the commandments have nothing to do with me; I have finished with them.' So they feel that in a sense it does not matter what they do, and they become lax and loose in their living and find themselves in trouble.

But John takes all this in a much more experimental and practical way, and we should thank him for it, because if you stop to think of it seriously, you will see that it is a complete error to say that the Christian has no relationship to the law. The law stands; 'Thou shalt not kill, thou shalt not steal . . .'—those laws have not been annulled. But Christians should be more than conquerors with respect to the law. John takes it for granted—indeed, he has been pursuing that very theme—that we love God by keeping His commandments, and these commandments are not only for the Jews, but for everybody. The Ten Commandments are the commandments of God to men and women at all times and in all places, and they have never been reduced or modified.

But John is much more concerned to be of help to us in a very practical sense, and this is his way of putting it. He tells us that in a sense the difference between the Christian and the non-Christian comes out more clearly, perhaps, with regard to this question of keeping the commandments than anywhere else. People are more likely to proclaim what they really are, whether they are Christians or not, by what they say about the commandments and what they do about them than in any other single respect. To the non-Christian, the commandments are very heavy. The commandments of God to non-Christians are a yoke; they feel they are a task and a burden, and in their heart of hearts they hate God because of this, and they would be very glad to be emancipated out of it all. But not to the Christian; His commandments, says John, are not a task and a terrible duty to the one who really is born again—His commandments are 'not grievous.'

So here is the test that we must all put to ourselves: what is our attitude to the commandments of God? Do I feel that the Christian life is a task, something against the grain, something to which I have to force and press myself? Do I merely attempt to keep the commandments because I am afraid not to; am I just playing for safety, or am I living this life because I enjoy it? Is it my desire to keep the commandments of God; do I recognise that they are essentially right, and do I long to conform to them increasingly? These are the questions, and it is my answer to them that really proclaim whether I am a Christian or not.

Now John, in a sense, helps us to discover all that; so let us summarise his teaching by putting it in the form of a number of propositions. The first, obviously, is this one: that which makes anybody feel that the commandments of God are grievous is the world. John

again introduces an argument for saying so: 'And his commandments are not grievous. For whatsoever is born of God overcometh
the world.' Now he has already been dealing with the subject of the
world, you remember, in the second chapter, where he has put it in
the form of a positive injunction: 'Love not the world, neither the
things that are in the world. If any man love the world, the love of
the Father is not in him. For all that is in the world, the lust of the
flesh, and the lust of the eyes, and the pride of life, is not of the
Father, but is of the world. And the world passeth away, and the lust
thereof: but he that doeth the will of God abideth for ever' (2:15-17).

That is, perhaps, one of the fullest statements in Scripture of
what the New Testament means by this term *the world*; here John
once more comes back to it. He is always very anxious about it, as
is every writer in the New Testament. You cannot read the New
Testament truly without seeing the whole of the Christian life as a
life of conflict; we are in an atmosphere and in a world where there
is a great fight going on. There are two kingdoms, the kingdom of
light and the kingdom of darkness, and you get these constant comparisons and contrasts. Paul says to the Ephesians, 'For we wrestle
not against flesh and blood, but against principalities, against powers, against the rulers of the darkness of this world, against spiritual wickedness in high places' (or 'in the heavenlies') (Eph 6:12).
'The world,' says John, 'is there the whole time, and the Christian
is fighting against it'; so it is of vital importance that we should
know what he means by this.

Perhaps the best way of defining what the New Testament
means by 'the world' is that it is everything that is opposed to God
and His Spirit. God calls upon men and women to worship Him
and to glorify Him; He calls upon them to live for His glory. There
is a famous quotation in the Shorter Catechism of the Westminster
Confession that says, 'The chief end of man is to glorify God and
to enjoy Him for ever.' That is the chief object for which God created us; we are meant to glorify God in every way conceivable. And
the world is everything that tries to prevent our doing that.

Now this is a very broad term, as we shall see, and I sometimes think there is nothing that is quite so pathetic as the case of those people who think that 'the world' just means worldly entertainment and nothing else. How pathetic that is in the light of the New Testament teaching! People fondly imagine that they have finished with the world just because they do not do certain things. But you may be as much in the world in the house of God as you are in a cinema or theatre, if you are proud of the fact that you are what you are and not what somebody else is, in that theoretical sense. The world, let me emphasise it again, is everything that stands between us and glorifying God only, utterly and absolutely.

The world, therefore, is something with which we have to reckon outside ourselves. So how do I confront it in that external sense? We cannot attempt to give an exhaustive answer here, so let me just give you some headings. The world does its best to prevent me from glorifying God by its attractions and its temptations. I need not elaborate on these, we are all well aware of them; they are everything that the world holds before us and with which it tries to appeal to us and that is calculated to draw us away from God. As we have seen, that is not the whole of what the world means, but it is a part of it.

But not only that, it is a person's outlook, for there are many people in the world today who would not dream of spending their time reading all the gruesome, detailed stories in the newspapers—they are too intelligent. But still, they may be as much a victim of the world as the other people who do spend their time doing that. The world is opposed to God in its outlook, in its mind, in its mentality, in its own wisdom—worldly wisdom. It is against God in its faith, in its own understanding, in its intellectualism that would banish God and ridicule the Cross and the blood of Christ, especially because it does not seem to be philosophically sound—all that is as much the world as the life of the gutter.

Even further, the world does its utmost to prevent us from glorifying God by persecuting us, and it has many ways of doing that.

Sometimes it does it by means of ridicule; it just laughs at us and makes us feel we are not intellectual. How often is this done in the office and in the profession, in the home, in the social contacts, and in various other places. And when ridicule does not succeed, it sometimes becomes isolation; you just find people drifting away. That is a terrible form of persecution, a very subtle and a very vicious one.

Sometimes persecution may even be physical. There are people—hundreds, not to say thousands, of men and women—who are being tempted by the devil, through this world, to deny God and to deny Christ. This is the position in which many find themselves if they go on proclaiming the gospel, or if they go on saying they believe it or continue to practise it. It may be that they will be thrown into prison and their wives and children will suffer; it may be that they will not be put into prison, but something will be done to the wife or the children. In whatever way, the world is trying to prevent their glorifying God. That is what we have to fight—the world outside us that manifests itself in those various ways.

But then there is also the world that is within us, and I put it like that because as we consider this I think we will see at a glance the whole error of monasticism. The world is outside, but, alas, it is also on the inside; the world is within me as well as without, and I have to fight on both fronts. The Apostle Paul says, 'The carnal mind is enmity against God: for it is not subject to the law of God, neither indeed can be' (Rom 8:7); so if I have a carnal mind, I am not glorifying God. A carnal mind is something that is inside me. Or again, he says to the Corinthians, 'We have received, not the spirit of the world, but the Spirit which is of God; that we might know the things that are freely given to us of God' (1 Cor 2:12).

The world, then, may be within me, that 'carnal mind' as the New Testament puts it. But what does that mean? Well, let us examine this foul, horrible thing that is in us as a result of the Fall and as a result of sin. There are two main manifestations of this. The first is *self* and everything that is covered by that little word. And what is self? First, it is pride; there is nothing perhaps that is quite so opposed to glorifying God as pride. It does not matter what you are proud of—your physical appearance, your mental ability, your position in life, your success. It does not matter what it is—any feeling of pride you may have is antagonism to God and makes it more difficult to glorify Him. Pride may take various forms: a desire for praise—we all know this—and a dislike of criticism, which is the negative counterpart. Then there is self-reliance, and this is perhaps one of the respects in which the modern world makes it most difficult for the modern man and woman to glorify God. It has been preaching self-reliance to us for so long: man, the master of his fate, the controller of his destiny; wonderful man, the discoverer of the secrets of the universe, harnessing nature. The popular books and the psychological teaching all suggest self-reliance, and the more you rely upon yourself, the less you trust God and the less you glorify Him and the less you live for Him.

And then, of course, there is ambition, a desire to get on and to succeed, in an unworthy sense; and selfishness, being anxious to have things for myself and for my own, not for somebody else and his own; and self-centredness and self-concern. Then out of that come jealousy and envy and coveting; a hardness in thought and a hardness in speech; unkindness; and all these other horrible things that you will find listed in certain passages of the New Testament. Paul has such a terrible list in the fifth chapter of Galatians (vv 17-21); read and examine yourself in the light of it.

Now, all these things are the world within me, and when they are in control and active, I am not glorifying God. When I am living for myself, I am concerned about myself in every shape and form. And then together with that self, there is the flesh; and when I say that, I mean appetites, desires, lusts—these things arise from within. We may be sitting by ourselves and suddenly an evil thought comes—it is the flesh, the desire of the flesh and of the mind. That is part of the world, and it is as opposed to glorifying God as are entertainments that are provided by the world outside us.

But it is not only that. One of the most terrible things the Christian has to fight is the flesh as it manifests itself in the form of indolence and a love of ease. There is a sense in which we are all lazy. Have you not often found yourself making excuses for not reading your Bible or praying? You would not think of making an excuse if you were going to read your newspaper; you would not think of ever making an excuse if it was a question of going to an entertainment; but when it is a question of going to a prayer meeting, it is too cold, or you are not feeling well—a thousand and one excuses come. The natural indolence of the flesh is all the time fighting against glorifying God, standing between us and the worship of God. There may be indolence, perhaps, even in the matter of sleep and in the matter of the distribution of our time. All these things come in, and they are a part of the world that is within us. Then there is a fear of softening, a fear of being a fool for Christ's sake; we all know this fear—it is a part of the flesh in us, this desire for ease. It is often, I believe, a lack of trust in God arising from the flesh.

But let me sum up like this: the world—and I think perhaps this is the best way of all to consider it—the world is everything outside me and within me and everywhere else that is doing its utmost to prevent me from conforming to the picture I find of the Christian in the Beatitudes in Matthew.

'Blessed are the poor in spirit'—the world will do its utmost to prevent your being poor in spirit by its praise, by its admiration, by suggesting to you how wonderful you are!

'Blessed are they that mourn'—the world will prevent your mourning because of your sin; it will laugh at you and say, 'Cheer up, all is well!' There is nothing the world hates so much as men and women who are prostrate before God because of their sinfulness and their unregenerate heart.

The Beatitudes are a description of what Christians are meant to be, and the world is doing everything it can to try to stop us, and it does this in the most subtle manner conceivable. It does it, as we have seen, in its suggestions to us. It is all opposed to this poverty of spirit that is the first condition, according to Christ Himself, and that is the high road that leads us to God and to fellowship with Him. The world is everything that is opposed to the message of the Beatitudes.

So the first principle is that it is the world that makes the commandments grievous. It is because we are fighting all that without and within that the commandments seem to be hard and heavy. Now the second principle involves the *relationship of the Christian to the world*, and the truth is that Christians do not conform to it; they have been commanded to be transformed and to be different. Christians not only do not conform to it, but they do not live as near to it as they can. That is the horrible temptation of sin. 'Well,' one might say, 'of course I don't want to be in this world; I want to be a Christian. So I will sit as near as I can to the border.' But that is not the Christian; the Christian does not just manage somehow or another not to go down. No; 'this is the victory that *overcometh* the world.' 'Whatsoever is born of God *overcometh* the world.' John uses that term three times in these two verses.

John means by that that the Christian is one who conquers the world, who masters it. He actually says a most extraordinary thing here, and for once I have to grant that the Revised Version is superior to the Authorised! The Authorised reads like this: 'And this is the victory that overcometh the world, even our faith.' But the Revised has, 'This is the victory that has overcome . . .'; it has already happened. Now John is saying two things here that at first sight, as so often with John, appear to be contradictory. He says that the Christian is one who has overcome the world and also that the Christian is one who overcomes the world. Christian people, John tells us, are men and women who are in an entirely new position with regard to this matter. They are not like the non-Christian, whom we have already been describing; Christians are in this new position because of their faith. They have come to see the real meaning of the world; they have come to see what it is, and they hate it. They know that the world has already been conquered by the Lord Jesus Christ, and they know that they themselves are in Christ; therefore, there is a sense in which the Christian has overcome the world. Christ has overcome it, and I am in Christ, and therefore I have overcome it.

And yet there is a sense in which I am still overcoming it; I am already victorious, but I still have to fight. The New Testament is very fond of saying that. 'But of him are ye in Christ Jesus,' says Paul, 'who of God is made unto us wisdom, and righteousness, and sanctification, and redemption' (1 Cor 1:30-31). He is already that to us; so there is a sense in which I am already sanctified, already glorified. Read the eighth chapter of Romans and you will find that Paul tells us that explicitly (vv 29-30); in Christ Jesus we are already complete, it has all happened. And yet I am also still being sanctified, and I am still on the way to glorification.

I wonder whether an illustration will help at this point. I am trying to say how at one and the same time it can be said that as Christians we have overcome *and* we are overcoming. Think of it in terms of the Battle of Quebec. General Wolfe conquered the French general Montcalm on the Heights of Abraham, and as the result of that battle Canada was conquered. And yet we read in our history books that the fight for possessing Canada went on for some seventy or eighty more years. That is it; the country was captured, and then captured in detail. Now the position of Christian men and women is something like that in this world. They are no longer under the dominion of Satan; they have been taken out of his kingdom, but that does not mean that they have finished with Satan.

Or look at it like this—think of it in terms of two big estates with a road going down between. On one side of the road there is one estate, and on the other side there is another; one of them is the kingdom of Satan, and the other is the kingdom of God. Now, this is what has happened to Christian men and women: they were in the estate under the dominion of Satan, but they have crossed over the road and are now in the kingdom of God. But though they are in this life and world, working in that new estate, the kingdom of God, Satan, their old enemy, is still there in that other kingdom, and he thinks that Christians will be foolish enough to listen to him. He forgets that they have been once and for ever taken out of his dominion; he forgets that they are free. So Christians do not come under his dominion, but they are still subject to his attacks and onslaughts and his suggestions and insinuations. They have overcome, but they are still fighting; they still have to overcome as they go on in this life walking with God and with Christ, walking in fellowship. They are overcoming increasingly; they no longer fall to the temptations that used to get them so easily, and thus they are no longer mastered by them.

But even further, those who are truly Christians are in the position of being able to say quite honestly that they do not want to sin. They do not want to, but still they do it; some things that remain in them from that old life still, as it were, get them down. This is what the Bible calls the flesh, the remains of the old man, and Christians hate it. They have overcome in that sense. They have got the victory, and yet they are not perfect; they have not arrived at sinless perfection. They are still tempted, and they still at times feel discouraged and almost defeated. And yet and yet . . . ! If they are true Christians, they know that they have the victory. They know that the crowning day is coming; they know that the day will dawn when they will be actually, in their walk, faultless and blameless and without spot, without rebuke, when they will be presented by their Lord and Saviour faultless before the presence of God's glory with exceeding joy.

4

Faith in Christ

For whatsoever is born of God overcometh the world: and
this is the victory that overcometh the world, even our
faith. Who is he that overcometh the world, but he that
believeth that Jesus is the Son of God?

1 JOHN 5:4-5

In our consideration of these verses, we have arrived at this position. There is a worldly mind and outlook and spirit with which
we are all afflicted by nature, and as long as we are governed by
that, the holy way of God is against us; we are opposed to it, and
we find it grievous. But according to John, what makes us Christian
is that the whole situation is transformed. Christians are those who
overcome the world; they have overcome it in a sense already and
are overcoming it, and we have emphasised that. But at the end
there still remained this question for us to consider, as to how it is
that the Christian is enabled to overcome. Now the Apostle is very
careful to tell us this, and here again we find how practical he is in
his exhortations and in all his writings. He does not merely tell us
that we overcome–he explains to us how we do so, and that makes
our victory still more sure.

This is a very great question. There is a sense in which it may
be said that the whole long history of the Christian Church is noth-

ing but the story and the history of two great rival views with regard to it. This whole problem of overcoming the world is a theme that has often been handled in the Church throughout the centuries, for anyone who is a Christian in any sense of the term must realise that there is this conflict. People who have no sense of conflict at all in their lives are patently just not Christians; they are in the sleep of death spiritually. The moment men and women become alive spiritually, they are aware of these forces and powers, and at once they are aware of a conflict. Those who do not realise that they are living in a world that is inimical to everything they hold to be true are not merely novices in these matters—I question whether they are in them at all. 'We wrestle not against flesh and blood,' says the Apostle Paul, and we cannot remind ourselves too often of this verse, 'but against principalities, against powers, against the rulers of the darkness of this world, against spiritual wickedness in high places' (Eph 6:12). That is it!

This, therefore, has been the great question: how is this world to be fought and to be conquered? Now, there have only been two main views with regard to this question, and we can classify them like this: there is what we may call the Catholic, or if you prefer it, the monastic view of this matter, and there is the evangelical view. I think that all the other views can be brought under one or the other of these two main headings. The Church has almost invariably been divided into one of these two groups. Let me say regarding the monastic or Catholic view, before I come to criticise it, that whatever we may say against monasticism, it at any rate has seen very clearly that the world is something that has to be fought. So there is a sense in which I would almost say that I would sooner have a monk or an anchorite who is separating himself from the world and dwelling in a cave or a hilltop because he realises he is in the fight of faith than a smug, glib, self-satisfied individual who has never realised there is a fight to be fought.

So let us look briefly at these two views. We shall favor the evangelical view, as I want to show you in these two verses of the Apostle

John; but let us look at it by way of contrast with this other view. The essence of the monastic or Catholic view of fighting the world is this: it believes in withdrawing from the world, but it also emphasises the exercise of willpower and the observance of a number of rules and regulations. The world, they say, is so active, so much with us—it is so insinuating—that the only thing to do is to come out of it, to withdraw from it. That is the essence of monasticism.

There are, therefore, those who have so felt the power of this teaching that they have not hesitated to leave their homes and their various professions and callings and businesses and have gone to places apart from the world. They have deliberately, in a physical sense, tried to go out of the world and have given themselves exclusively to what they call 'the religious life.' They have spent their time in meditation, in prayer, and in thought, and invariably they have prescribed for themselves, or have had prescribed for them, various rules and orders. They have believed in fasting, in the literal sense, twice a week, sometimes more; they have their times and seasons, such as Lent, when they deny themselves and the flesh and the body in various respects. So that is what is meant by this monastic view; you must go out of the world, and by means of rigorous discipline and practices in various respects, you thus attempt to fight and to overcome that world that is doing its utmost to destroy your soul and to stand between you and God.

What, then, have we to say to that view? Well, there are three main things. There has always seemed to me to be one difficulty about it that is more than sufficient to put it out of court, and that is that it is clearly something that all cannot do. There is a sense in which you have to be a very special kind of person before you can practise that kind of life; so it seems to me to fail at that point because it gives the average and ordinary Christian no hope. Now, the way in which they overcome that difficulty is to divide Christians into two groups: those who have to remain in the world, in business or occupation—the ordinary; and the extraordinary, who have taken up the religious life as a vocation and make it a full-time matter. And their teaching, of course, is that those 'religious' people, as they call them, not only acquire sufficient merit for themselves—they also acquire a superabundance of merit. Therefore, they pray to them as saints and ask them for supererogation in order to make up for their own deficiency.

Now I think that by that teaching they are virtually granting that there is something essentially wrong about their whole concept of overcoming the world. It is only for certain select persons, it is not something that the average Christian can practise, and therefore it seems to me it is utterly unscriptural, for there is no such division and distinction between Christians in the New Testament. The Apostles put themselves in with everybody else; these things are preached to all Christians, and not only to a select few.

But there is something else that is equally marked, and here we must see where this view is so superficial. The tragedy with this view, as I see it, is that it forgets entirely that the world is not only outside me, but inside me. We were at pains to emphasise that earlier when we saw that the world is not only outside us with its sin and temptations and attractions, but it is also inside us—the flesh, our own unregenerate nature. So in a sense, it is almost childish to think that I can overcome the world by taking myself out of it, because when I have gone into my cell the world is still within me; so my attempt to escape by physical means is almost doomed to failure. This is something that we all must know from experience. We have all been alone, we have all been isolated at certain times; the world has not been there to tempt us. But was all well with us? Were we perfectly happy; were we free from temptation; was the mind and the outlook and the spirit of the world entirely absent? God knows that such is not the case!

Let me give you a story to illustrate this. I was reading of a saint who lived in Scotland some 250 years ago. He was a farmer, and this man, as the result of a sermon preached one Sunday, had felt very definitely and acutely that he must conquer the self within him. This became such a burden to him that he decided he would spend a whole day alone on the top of a mountain near his house in fasting and prayer in order that once and for ever he might deal with this fiend, this self. So he went up to the top of the mountain, and he spent the day there in struggle, in anguish, and in prayer pleading with God to rid him of this foul thing.

Then towards the afternoon and early evening, at last he felt he had obtained his victory—he felt he had been delivered completely. God seemed to have delivered him from self, and he was filled with a spirit of joy and elation. So he spent some further time in rejoicing and praising God. But then he began to descend the mountain and to go home for the evening, and just as he was coming to the foot of the mountain he saw some of his neighbours just finishing the day's work of carting in the hay. And as he looked at these people who had thus been toiling wearily throughout the day, he found himself saying to himself, 'How much better have I spent the day than they have been doing! While they have been attending to these material, mechanical, earthly things, I have been giving my attention to the soul!' In other words, he found in that moment that the enemy he thought he had finished with once and for ever on the top of the mountain was still inside him.

You can go away and spend your day on the top of a mountain, but you cannot get away from the world; it is in you, so that any retirement to a monastery, or becoming an anchorite or a hermit, is doomed to failure. That is the whole story of Martin Luther; look at that excellent monk in his cell—fasting, sweating, praying; out of the world in a sense, and yet finding that the world was in him and he could get no peace. Therefore, withdrawal from the world and from society does not get rid of the world in the New Testament sense of the term.

In other words, and this is my third objection to it, the monastic view is thoroughly unscriptural; there is no such teaching to be found in the New Testament, and especially when you look at the life of our Lord Himself. Here was one who had overcome the world, and yet, you observe, He did not do so by segregating

Himself from the world. He was in the world, and He mixed with the common people; indeed, He was misunderstood because of that. The Pharisees looked at Him and said, 'He cannot be a prophet—He is the friend of publicans and sinners; He does not segregate Himself.' There we see, once and for all, not only in our Lord's teaching and the teaching of the whole of the New Testament, but in His example also, that the way to overcome the world is not just mechanical; it is not a question of withdrawal.

So having glanced briefly at the monastic or Catholic view, let us now contrast it with what I have described as the evangelical view, which, I claim, we are entitled to call the biblical view. How do Christians arrive at the position in which they overcome the world? Well, as I see it here, the Apostle says there are two main things in answer to this question. The first is that they do so because of what has happened to them, because of what is true of them as Christians. And the second is that they do so because of what their faith in Christ enables them to do.

Now let us look at that first principle. Christians, we have seen, are those who overcome; there is a sense in which they have already overcome, and they are still overcoming. But how do they do it? Well, there is nothing here that tells them they have taken up the religious life, so-called, as a vocation; there is nothing about going behind a wall and then putting regulations and rules on the wall and keeping them day by day. Nothing of the kind! First and foremost we are told of certain things that are true of us as Christians; something has happened to us, and it is because of this that we can thus overcome.

What are these things? First, Christians overcome the world because they are born, or begotten, of God: 'Whatsoever is born of God overcometh the world.' Now once more I would call your attention to the order in which the Apostle puts these things. He puts first the new birth; then second, and only second, faith; and thirdly, a particular faith in the Lord Jesus Christ and our relationship to Him. These are points of interest theologically; they are not vital to salvation, but if we want our minds to be clear, we must observe the Apostle's order.

Now, if we are begotten of God this, of course, means that we start with a new disposition, a new outlook, and there you see the fundamental distinction between the Catholic and the evangelical view of this question. Because the Catholic view fails to emphasise this rebirth and regeneration as it should, it has to take us out of the world mechanically and has to impose its list of rules and regulations. But the evangelical view comes and tells us, 'You need not come out of the world; what you need is a new view of it; what you need is new outlook upon it.' It is, in other words, something like this: the whole trouble, says the New Testament, is not so much the world itself as the spirit that is in you and the view you take. I remember once reading a phrase that can be applied to this point: it is not life that matters, but the courage that we bring to it. Now, I am not interested in the courage, but I am interested in the outlook; it is not the world really that accounts for our failure—it is ourselves.

Is this not obvious the moment you begin to think of it? Look at two men walking down the street. One is a saint, the other is a worldling—and what a vital contrast between the two men! There is one sense in which the two men are absolutely different, and yet they are living in exactly the same world, the same surroundings, the same sin, the same temptations, the same everything. So what is the difference? The difference is in the men and not in the world.

> Two men looked out through prison bars.
> The one saw mud and the other stars.

Two men in the same prison look out through the same bars on the same world and see two entirely different things. 'Beauty is in the eye of the beholder'; it is not the world that matters—it is the way in which we look at it.

Now, that is the vital teaching of the New Testament; it is the

essence of the evangelical position. It involves being able to look at
the world as the Lord Jesus Christ looked at it, and that is the whole
meaning of being born again. That is the essence of this doctrine—
it is the teaching with regard to the rebirth. We have become, as
Peter puts it, 'partakers of the divine nature' (2 Pet 1:4); we have
received the disposition of God Himself. We look at things from the
Godward angle rather than from the human and carnal and sinful
one. What a wonderful doctrine this is, and how it shows the foolishness of that rival view! Where I am, exactly where I am without
moving an inch, my whole outlook can be different. Therein I see
a hope that puts me right; it puts me right essentially, internally, so
that in spite of the world, which remains the same, I am a different
person in that world, and I am now in a position to overcome it.
That is the first principle.

The second principle is that as a Christian, because of what has
happened to me, I am able to exercise faith and to live by faith. Here
is the second step. First you see 'Whatsoever is born of God overcometh the world,' and then 'This is the victory that overcometh
the world, even our faith.' In other words, my rebirth gives me this
faculty of faith and enables me to exercise faith and to live by it. Let
me put it in this practical form: the world that I am fighting is very
powerful; it is much more powerful than any one of us. The world
conquers and masters everyone who is born into it, for indeed we
have been born in sin and shapen in iniquity (Psa 51:5); the world
is in us the moment we begin to live. Read your Old Testament;
look at those great heroes of the faith, the patriarchs, the godly
kings and the prophets—they all were conquered by the world, they
all failed. 'There is none righteous, no, not one' (Rom 3:10); the
whole world is guilty before God (Rom 3:19); and, therefore, if I
am to conquer and overcome that world, I need something that will
enable me to do so. It is no use trying to fight the world immediately—that cannot be done. Monasticism recognises that and says,
'Run away from it.'

So what do I need? I need emancipation; I need to be lifted to another realm; I need a force and a strength and a power that I have not got myself. That is my need, and here is the answer: I am given a faith—I am given an outlook and understanding—I am introduced to a source of power—I see something that that other person has never seen. I see beyond. I see a might and a power that is even greater than all that is opposed to me. Now that again, you will agree, is the essence of the New Testament teaching. Christians are men and women who have been introduced to another realm. There is another dimension in their lives; there is a power in them and available to them that they had never known before and that no one who is outside of Christ can possibly know. So here are people who have this new nature and outlook, this new disposition and understanding. And that, in turn, is something that enables them to be linked to that other realm.

But let me put it still more specifically, for John goes on to a third step: 'Who is he,' he says, 'that overcometh the world, but he that believeth that Jesus is the Son of God?' That is it—that is everything. The thing, in other words, that makes Christian men and women overcome the world, and enables them to do so, and to do so increasingly, is their relationship to the Lord Jesus Christ, to His work and what He has accomplished and already finished. That is the whole of the evangelical position with regard to this matter. It is not just carrying out a number of rules, nor is it willpower; it is none of these things. We find Paul denouncing this in Colossians 2, where he is dealing with exactly the same idea, this monastic idea. In those New Testament times there were people observing their holy days, and they were doing this, that, and the other. 'It is of no avail,' says Paul, 'it is all of the flesh; it is the old and not the new.'

And in that entire chapter the Apostle's argument is that all that kind of thing is not only wrong but unnecessary; and it is unnecessary because everything we need is in the Lord Jesus Christ—'in him dwelleth all the fulness of the Godhead bodily.' In Him we are 'complete.' 'He is the Head,' says Paul in effect, 'and everything comes out of Him. There is no need for your philosophies or your false ascetisms. There is no need for this mutilation of the body, nor for these mechanical attempts to conquer the world; it is unnecessary. Everything you need is in Christ.' And John is here simply saying exactly that. He puts it in the form of a question: 'Who is he that overcometh the world?' 'Well,' he says, 'he is the man who believes that Jesus is the Son of God; he has seen who Christ is and what He has done, and he is drawing on that perfect, finished work.'

But let me end by putting it again in the memorable phrase of the Apostle Paul. He tells us, 'I live; yet not I, but Christ liveth in me: and the life which I now live in the flesh I live by the faith of the Son of God' (Gal 2:20)–by this faith in the Son of God, by this relationship to Him 'who loved me, and gave himself for me.'

That is the principle that we have to grasp. We shall work out those principles in still further and greater detail, but the vital thing for us is this matter of our relationship to Christ. If I am not in that right relationship, then nothing else can happen; but if I am in the right relationship, then, says the Apostle, everything can happen. Because if I am rightly related to Him, I shall draw from Him; and what makes me rightly related to Him is that I am born again. It is only as I receive this new life, this new birth, that I am able to recognise Him, that I am able to believe in Him, that I am able to exercise faith in Him, that I am able to rest on Him and receive and draw of His fulness. It is this matter of the new birth that relates me to Him, for I am born of Him and I receive of His nature.

So then, that is the principle in which we stand as Evangelicals. I need not try to run out of this world; I need not spend the whole of my life doing things and trying to mortify my flesh. I need not go out of my business or profession, or retire from the world into some cell; I need not conform to mechanical rules that appear to give me temporary satisfaction. No; the essential thing is that my whole outlook upon this world should be different, not only at certain times and seasons, but always; not only on a Sunday, but every day. I, having a new mind and disposition, a new outlook, have seen the world for what is it.

But thank God, I have also seen much more. I have seen the life that is in Christ and the life that is possible to me in Him. I am related to Him; I live by faith in Him and draw from Him the power that is more than sufficient to master and to conquer this world both without and within, everything that is opposed to the highest interest of my soul. Thank God that whether I am in the midst of life, at home or on the street or at work, wherever I am, whatever may be opposed to me with circumstances all against me—in spite of all that, because of what is within me, I can triumph and I can prevail. 'Whatsoever is born of God overcometh the world.'

5
How Faith Overcomes

For whatsoever is born of God overcometh the world: and this is the victory that overcometh the world, even our faith. Who is he that overcometh the world, but he that believeth that Jesus is the Son of God?

1 JOHN 5:4-5

We have seen that what really makes it possible to overcome the world is the fact that because we are born again we are vitally and intimately connected to the Lord Jesus Christ. It is our relationship to Him that enables us to overcome; and we can sum it up by saying that it is indeed our faith in Christ that makes victory over the world a practical, actual possibility. So what we must do now is to work out in detail how this relationship of the Christian to Jesus Christ works out in practice; how is it that this faith of ours in the Lord Jesus Christ, this belief that He is the Son of God and all the consequences that follow from that belief, enables us thus in practice to overcome the world.

Now this is very important in the Christian life. It is the whole secret of successful living; it is the whole secret of joy.

So we must consider it, and the best way of dividing up this sub-

ject is to divide it into two main headings. This faith of ours that
enables us to overcome the world does so directly and also indirectly—or if you prefer, in a passive manner and in an active manner. Or to put it in still another way, we can say that it does so by
the exercise of naked faith and also by meditation upon and working out, even intellectually or in the understanding, the meaning
and the implications of faith. Let us, then, look at these two.

First of all, faith enables us to have a victory over the world and
to overcome it directly—passively—by the resting of a naked faith
upon the Lord Jesus Christ. I start with that because I am indeed
increasingly convinced that it is the greatest lesson that as Christian
people we can ever learn in this world. It is the possibility of directly
and immediately and passively resting upon the power and the ability of our risen Lord. 'This is the victory that overcometh the world,
even our faith'—my faith in Him, my belief in Him, that He is the
Son of God. The result of that is that I go to Him and rest upon
Him.

This is something that you will find enunciated everywhere in
the Bible. Let me give you just one quotation that will illustrate it
perfectly and represent all others: 'The name of the Lord is a strong
tower; the righteous runneth into it and is safe' (Prov 18:10). That
is it! Read the various Psalms, too, and see how those godly men
of old were struggling against the world and its temptations and
insinuations, and they will all tell you that that was the only thing
they could do. They did not attempt to battle. They saw that the
forces were too great for them. They might have failed, but they
said, 'There is only one thing to do; I will run into the tower, and
there in the tower I am safe.'

Or if you like it in New Testament form, it is the doctrine of the
vine and the branches, as seen in the statement of our Lord:
'Without me ye can do nothing' (John 15:5). It is put positively by
the Apostle Paul: 'I can do all things through Christ which strength-
eneth me' (Phil 4:13); and, 'nevertheless I live; yet not I, but Christ
liveth in me' (Gal 2:20). All those phrases are merely expressions

of this first and all-important way of obtaining the victory that over-comes the world through faith in Christ. It means, in other words, turning to Christ, flying to Him–hiding in Him, looking to Him in a literal sense for protection, defence, and deliverance–relying utterly upon Him.

This is what I would call the simplicity of faith, and yet it is one of the most difficult lessons to learn. Most of our defeats, I think, are due to the fact that we parley with sin, we attempt to fight it. Now there is a sense in which we have to do that, and that will be my second heading when we come to deal with faith indirectly. But what I am concerned to emphasise here is that before you attempt to do the second you must do the first. There are times in our experience when, for reasons often beyond our own control, unless we run to Christ and hide in Him we are certain to be defeated. But thank God, the possibility that is held up before us is that we can go to Him directly, immediately and look to Him. This is what I might call 'the great strategy of faith'; we need to know when to do that and to realise that is something always open and possible to us.

So the rest of faith, in a sense, means just this, that there are times when we do not even attempt to fight this battle against sin and must simply look to Christ. Perhaps an illustration will make my point clear. I once read a little pamphlet that was very simple but that, it seemed to me, shared the whole essence of this particular aspect of the doctrine. It was the story of a Christian in South Africa, travelling out in the country, and he came to an agricultural community. Owing to certain floods in the country, he had to stay where there was a kind of saloon or public house. He was amazed and saddened at the sight of the farmers, many of whom, he noticed, came there and spent in a few days all the money that they had been able to earn and save as the result of their hard work through the year. They had a powerful craving for drink that they could not conquer.

He was especially attracted to one poor man who seemed to be a particular victim to this terrible affliction, and he began to talk to him. First of all he began to reason with him, pointing out the suffering that his wife and children had to endure. The poor man admitted it all and told the story of how he had been almost unconsciously led into it and found himself a helpless slave to drink before realising that anything had happened—how he would give the whole world if he could stop it, but he was now a victim of it. Then this Christian went on to tell him about faith, the possibility of overcoming, and told him about the Lord Jesus Christ who had come into this world to save us. He told him that if only he looked to Christ and relied upon Him, he would be enabled to overcome this thing, and the man was given faith to believe that. He was a simple, illiterate man, and all he was anxious to do was to find the name of this person about whom this Christian was speaking, and he was told the name was Jesus.

The story went on to say how that poor man went away and, having worked again, came back to this same place to sell his grain. There again the tempters came, but he did not go with them, and his own wife and children were amazed. This Christian visitor came back in a year or so to find the man entirely changed. He began talking to him and asked him how it had happened. And the man's simple testimony was this: 'I went back the first time, and my friends came and tempted me, and I felt weak. But suddenly I remembered the name—Jesus. I could do nothing but keep on saying to myself, "Jesus"; I cried to Jesus to do what you told me He would do.' His faith was as simple as that, but it was enough, and he overcame; he did not go back, he was emancipated.

That is what I mean when I talk about this direct faith; it is simply resting upon Christ, and I have to do that. That is 'becoming as a little child,' realising our utter weakness and helplessness and hopelessness. And when the fight is yet strong and the enemy is there and we feel we are on the point of falling, we must simply cry, 'Jesus' and believe and know that He is looking on and that He is there and is ready to deliver us and protect us. 'The name of the Lord is a strong tower, the righteous runneth into it and is safe.'

There are times in Christian experience when that is the only thing to do. You just realise that the Lord is there. You just sing or say the hymn:

I need Thee every hour;
Stay thou near by;
Temptations lose their power
When Thou art nigh.

Annie Sherwood Hawks

And then we must just realise by faith that He is there, ever at hand, mighty to save. As little children, we look to Him; we abandon ourselves to Him. We do not look at the enemy; we simply look to Him and rely upon Him. We fly into His almighty arms, and as certainly as we do so, He will protect us, He will save us, He will deliver us with 'the peace of God, which passeth all understanding' (Phil 4:7), He will garrison and hold us.

In a sense that is the great story of every Christian confessor and saint throughout the centuries. What hope, do you think, is there for those to whom the gospel is preached who may never have had any education and who may be victims of subtle temptations of the flesh and of the mind? How are these people to emancipate themselves? What is the use of preaching moral uplift under such conditions? There is only one answer as to the way in which men and women can be changed; it is the power of this risen living Christ to deliver them in their utter hopelessness and helplessness. Whosoever looks to Him will be delivered.

That therefore is the victory that overcomes the world in that passive sense—just simple, utter reliance, in our weakness, upon Him, upon the power of His might. There is a great hymn by Lavacer which expresses it all perfectly. Read something about him, that Swiss Christian man of the last century. He had proved in experience everything he wrote in that hymn, and I urge, in the hour of temptation when the enemy is powerful and strong, that we just repeat it:

> *O Jesus Christ, grow Thou in me*
> *And all things else recede.*
> *Each day let Thy supporting might*
> *My weakness still embrace.*

That is it.

> *Let faith in Thee and in Thy might*
> *My every motive move.*

Victory is only in Him, in His might, and not in myself; this comes with the realisation of my own weakness and the realisation of His almighty power, and simply abandoning myself to Him. Let me say it again: 'the name of the Lord is a strong tower'; the righteous runs into it when the enemy is after him, and he is 'safe.' The enemy cannot enter; the Lord will protect him.

My second division is the indirect or what I have described alternatively as *active*, and which I have also described as the working out of this faith. This is something that is again of tremendous importance, as long as we put it in the second place. It is here I see the glorious nature of our Christian position. In our utter helplessness, when we seem to be incapable of rising or going on, when we see this powerful enemy coming and feel that we are on the point of sinking, we flee. But it is not always like that, thank God! As one goes on in the Christian life, one ought to be working out this indirect method. This is the activity of faith, the thinking out of the Christian gospel and of what faith in Christ really means. It means to understand what we really mean when we say that 'Jesus is the Son of God.' It means working out the implication of that in terms of this fight of ours against the world and the flesh and the devil, and I suggest that this working out means something like this:

First of all, as I look at the Lord Jesus Christ in terms of this fight against the world, I ask this question: why did He ever come into this world? You see I am now working out my faith in Christ. I believe that the person, Jesus of Nazareth, about whom I read in the Gospels, is the Son of God. Very well, I ask immediately, why did the Son of God ever take upon Himself the likeness of sinful flesh and live as man, as He indeed did? What is the meaning of it all? And there is only one answer to that question. It was because of the power of sin, the power of Satan, the power of evil. There is no other explanation. The Son of God came because He was the only way in which we could be delivered from the world.

In other words, it is the doctrine of sin again, the power of Satan and sin and evil. He came into this world because the world was dominated by sin, and it is only as I believe that 'Jesus is the Son of God' that I begin to understand the nature of the fight in which I am engaged. People are optimistic about this world, and they are so because they have never understood the nature of sin. But if you believe that Jesus is the Son of God, you have to believe that the power of sin and evil and Satan is so tremendous that man had failed and the Son of God had to come.

Do you see, then, how this enables us to overcome the world? How can I overcome the world unless I have seen the nature of the problem? But the moment I have faith in Christ, I begin to understand it, for it is only the Christian who can see through this world. Everybody else is dominated by the world—governed by it. Do you not see it around and about you? Look at the newspapers and you will see it. People think that life is wonderful and that the world is a marvellous place. They have never seen through it; they are entirely deluded by its so-called glittering prizes. How they vie with one another in their so-called enjoyments and in their efforts to gain certain positions; oh, the excitement of it all! What is the matter with them? Ah, the tragedy is that they have never seen through it; they are just duped by it. But the moment I become a Christian I see through the world.

This is tremendously significant and is of great practical importance for the Christian. Let me put it in this form to call your attention to it: I would say, for an example, that by definition Christians
must never become too excited about politics,[1] and for this reason,
that they know perfectly well that there is no solution to the ultimate problem of mankind in politics. So people who believe that,
as a result of a win for one party rather than another at an election
everything is going to be fundamentally different—those people are
either not Christians or else they are very ignorant ones. No; nothing that can happen at an election will touch this problem. The par-
ties are all equally in sin; they are all under the domination of sin.

Now, Christians should be concerned about these things; they
have a duty as citizens, and let them exercise it. But if they become
excited, if they believe that one rather than the other is going to
make the vital difference, they have never seen the truth about the
world. Men and women who believe that 'Jesus is the Son of God'
have seen through the world; they know that no Acts of Parliament
can solve the problem of mankind. They look on, therefore, objec-
tively. There is a detachment about them; they are looking at it
from the outside. They do not pin their faith upon it, for they see
beyond it. They see the fate of all those who are dominated by the
world; they know that all who belong to the world, in this New
Testament sense, are going to perdition and damnation. They see
through it all, and they know that none but Christ can deliver them
from it. That is the first thing.

Secondly, the men and women who believe that 'Jesus is the
Son of God' look at the New Testament records, and there they see
this Jesus of Nazareth, and they see Him overcoming the world.
They see Him tempted by Satan and conquering him; they see
Satan giving up; they see one who at last can take the strong man
armed and take his goods from him. They look at this perfect life
in which there was no blot or blemish; they see Him literally meeting hell at its worst in mortal combat and overcoming it. What a
difference this makes! They have read the Old Testament also and

have seen that everybody had been defeated by Satan—not a single person had conquered. But at last here is one who conquers Satan, and they see Him conquering in His life, in His death, and in His glorious resurrection. They see in the resurrection that even the last enemy has been conquered; the last thing that Satan could do to bind men and women and hold them has been utterly defeated. So here again is something that enables me to overcome. As I attempt to face the problems of life and to overcome the world, I am aware of my own weakness and all those forces that are against me. But my outlook is immediately changed when I look at Christ and see that He has overcome it.

But the next step is this: by faith I see myself belonging to Christ. I am 'in Christ'—that is the New Testament phrase. As the branch is in the vine, so I am in Christ. I belong; I am a part of Him. I am incorporated in Him. And, of course, if that is true, I am a sharer in everything that belongs to Him; I am already a sharer in His victory. We are told here by John, as we have seen, that the Christian has already overcome, in a sense: 'Whatsoever is born of God *has overcome* the world.' I have done so in Christ. He has overcome, I am in Him, and therefore I have overcome; and at once, again, my whole attitude towards the fight is changed.

But that works out a little more practically in this way, in that it enables me to see that I can literally draw strength and power from Him and from His fulness. John in his Gospel says, 'And of His fulness have all we received, and grace for [or upon] grace' (John 1:16). I have illimitable resources behind me; I have a source of supply that can never fail. 'He that cometh to me shall never hunger; and he that believeth on me shall never thirst' (John 6:35). These are absolutes; there is literally no limit to the power of Christ. In Him are treasured all the resources of the Godhead; 'in him dwelleth all the fulness of the Godhead bodily' (Col 2:9). I am in Him, and I can therefore draw upon Him; I care not what forces are against me when I remember this power that is behind me and within me.

But let me go still another step to show you how practical this is—I am still working out this faith. There are times when I fail because in my folly I do not run into the strong tower, because I try to fight in my own strength, and the enemy defeats me. There are times when I go down. Now this is most important. At that particular point there is nothing that is so liable to happen to me as that the enemy will come and say something like this to me: 'Ah, well, you have failed—you have fallen. You have sinned against the Lord. You have gone back. What is the use of talking about your faith—look at yourself!' And there I am, overwhelmed with a sense of failure and frustration, and I wonder whether I have a right to turn to God and to pray. I have let myself down, I have let God down, I have let Christ down; and I feel utterly hopeless with a sense of despair and futility.

Now there is nothing more precious at that point than to know that Jesus is the Son of God and that He tells me that though I have sinned, though I have failed, as we have already found it in this epistle,[2] 'If we confess our sins, he is faithful and just to forgive us our sins, and to cleanse us from all unrighteousness' (1:9). 'My little children, these things write I unto you, that ye sin not. And if any man sin, we have an advocate with the Father, Jesus Christ the righteous: and he is the propitiation for our sins: and not for yours only, but also for the sins of the whole world' (2:1-2). There is nothing, then, that so enables me to overcome as that deliverance from sins and failure, from that sense of despair that tends to overwhelm me when I feel I have gone down and cannot rise again. The blood of Christ will cleanse me, and I rise up and go forward on my journey.

But, lastly, faith enables me to see the ultimate glory and perfection that await me. The fight in this world often seems long and endless, and we tend to become tired and weary. There is nothing that so encourages me as to realise that the day is certainly coming when I shall be ultimately glorified and perfect, without spot or wrinkle or blemish; when Christ, who has died for me and sustained me, will present me faultless before the presence of the glory of God with exceeding joy. Does that not help you to fight? Does it not help you to know that the victory is secure, that the crowning day is coming, that you shall see Him as He is and be delivered entirely from everything that could hold you down? This is a vision by faith of the ultimate glory that awaits us, the coming again of the Son of God, 'who shall change our vile body, that it may be fashioned like unto his glorious body, according to the working whereby he is able even to subdue all things unto himself' (Phil 3:21).

So let me sum it all up by putting it like this: this is how faith overcomes—I fly to Christ in utter helplessness, but I also work faith out. I reason out the implication of believing that 'Jesus is the Son of God'; and fortified by all these things, I overcome and am enabled to overcome. I triumph, and I find that the commandments of God are no longer 'grievous.'

I end with a simple question: are you overcoming; or are you weary of the fight? The Christian is one, according to the New Testament, who does overcome. If I cannot say, therefore, that I am overcoming the world in these various ways, I had better examine the very foundation of my position once more. 'Whatsoever is born of God overcometh the world: and this is the victory that overcometh the world, even our faith. Who is he that overcometh the world, but he that believeth that Jesus is the Son of God?'

6

The God-Man

This is he that came by water and blood, even Jesus Christ;
not by water only, but by water and blood. And it is the
Spirit that beareth witness, because the Spirit is truth. For
there are three that bear record in heaven, the Father, the
Word, and the Holy Ghost: and these three are one. And
there are three that bear witness in earth, the spirit, and the
water, and the blood: and these three agree in one.

1 JOHN 5:6-8

Here again we come to one of those points of transition that,
as I have reminded you many times, is one of the characteristic features, from the standpoint of literary structure
and logical order of thought, that characterised this Apostle.
Indeed, we have already arrived at that point of transition at the end
of the fifth verse: 'Who is he that overcometh the world, but he that
believeth that Jesus is the Son of God?' Already you can see in one
verse that John is leaving the particular subject of overcoming the
world—which was a part of his consideration of keeping the commandments—and has come to one of his other major themes,
namely, the correctness of doctrine with respect to the person of our
Lord and Saviour Jesus Christ.

Now we have seen that it is an essential part of John's method to hold certain arguments constantly before us, and you remember we pointed out how he does this in a kind of circular fashion. There are certain things, he says, that are essential to the Christian position, and we must hold them and practise them all together and at the same time: love of God, keeping His commandments, love for the brethren, and a correct doctrine about the person of the Lord Jesus Christ. And we have seen how in the epistle, right away from the beginning to the point that we have now reached, he keeps on playing on these four points. Each one leads to the other, so that it does not matter with which one we start, we seem to arrive at all the others. And here is another illustration of that very thing. In dealing with the doctrine of the commandments and the keeping of the commandments, which he puts in terms of overcoming the world, he has arrived at this further doctrine of a correctness of view with regard to the person of Christ.

Obviously, this is something that is of central importance. If the whole basis of my victory and my overcoming the world is that I have faith in Christ and lean upon Him, and if am to I look to Him and rely upon Him, then it is important for me to know that I *can* rely upon Him. If I am going to risk the whole of my life and my whole outlook upon this particular reliance, then I must be absolutely certain about it. You must be sure of your foundation before you begin to erect your building; you must be right about first principles before you can put in the details. And that is how John quite naturally comes to verses 6, 7, and 8. He is talking about Jesus the Son of God; the one who 'came by water and blood, even Jesus Christ.' And now from verse 6 right until the end of verse 12 John is really concerned about this doctrine of the person of Christ. If I am in any doubt at all about Him, then of course there is no prospect whatsoever of my overcoming the world. I must be absolutely certain of this; I must be absolutely right about Him.

The whole of the Christian position rests entirely upon this doctrine. There is no such thing as Christianity apart from Him. To be a Christian does not only mean to believe in God. The ortho-

dox Jew believes in God, and so do Mohammedans; and there are
many others who believe in Him. The thing that makes Christians
Christian is that they believe that Jesus is the Son of God. In this
matter of their knowledge of God and their relationship to Him,
they rest entirely upon the Lord Jesus Christ.

That is why we say that there must be absolute certainty at this
point, because the New Testament does not offer us anything at all
apart from Him. Indeed, I can say that about the whole Bible. The
Old Testament saints were all looking forward to Him. Everything
points to Him; everything centres upon Him, so that there must be
no querying and questioning. And John, teacher as he was, comes
back to it once more. He has already dealt with it several times, but,
you see, the man really knows himself and human nature as the
result of sin. He knows that you have to go on saying these things
because we are so prone to forget them and to slip or slide back into
some wrong way of thinking. Heresies and errors came into the
early church almost at once; how easy it would be to go astray! And
John, knowing that he is an old man, says, 'I cannot take any risk
about this. We must be certain as to this question, because without
Him there is no hope whatsoever of overcoming the world.'

So this is the theme from verses 6 to 12; and as I understand it,
he divides this up into three main divisions. First of all, you have
in verses 6, 7 and 8 what I am describing as the testimony of Jesus
Christ and His person. In verses 9 and 10 you have reasons given
as to why we should accept the testimony. And in verses 11 and 12
we have the consequences of accepting the testimony—what happens to me as the result of so doing.

Let us, then, look at this first section: the testimony or the witness that is borne to the Lord Jesus Christ; how I may know that
He really is one on whom I can rely. Now there can be no question
at all but that these three verses are not only the most difficult verses
in this epistle, but I think I am prepared to say that they are the three
most difficult verses, in a sense, in the entire Bible! And anybody
who has ever read commentaries and books that deal with this mat-

ter will agree with what I am saying, because the moment you look
at them you are confronted by an initial difficulty. The sixth verse
of the Authorised Version (King James Version) reads, 'This is he
that came by water and blood, even Jesus Christ; not by water only,
but by water and blood'; then verse 7 reads, 'For there are three that
bear record in heaven, the Father, the Word, and the Holy Ghost:
and these three are one.' That is not in the other versions. Verse 8
in the Authorised Version reads, 'And there are three that bear witness in earth, the spirit, and the water, and the blood: and these
three agree in one.' The Revised and other versions read something
like this for verses 7 and 8: 'For there are three that bear record, the
Spirit and the water and the blood, and these three agree in one.'
There is nothing in the Revised Version about the three that bear
record in heaven and the three that bear record on earth; so at once,
of course, we are confronted by a problem—why this difference?

    In a sense this is just a question of mechanics, and yet in its way
it is of some importance, and the answer is that this is purely a question of what is called textual criticism. I do not want to spend time
on this, and yet I do believe that if we want to read the Bible intel-
ligently we must know something about this. John wrote this epistle, but we do not actually possess a copy of what John himself
wrote; the original manuscripts and documents are not in the possession of the Church. They were written, and then a number of
copies were made of these various letters and books; but the original documents somehow or another disappeared. But there are
large numbers of manuscripts extant that are copies in various lan-
guages of these original documents; you have them in Greek and
Latin, in Coptic and in the Abyssinian language.

    Those have been current and in existence, of course, for cen-
turies. Now, the Authorised Version is a translation of a Greek text
of the New Testament that dates from the twelfth century A.D. It
was published by the great Erasmus in the sixteenth century, and
it is virtually the text from which this Authorised Version was produced and translated in 1611. The Revised Version is a translation

dating from about 1880. That translation was not new. By this time a great deal of research had been going on, and as a result of a lot of drafting, the schools were generally agreed that they now had what might be considered the text that approximated more nearly to the original lost documents. We need not go into this; it is purely a question of textual research. But the result was that a text was produced that is commonly known as the text of Westcott and Hort, and it was from them that the translation was made for the Revised Version. And thus you see there is a difference between the Revised and the Authorised with regard to these particular statements about the witness in heaven and the witness on earth.

But let me go still a step further with regard to that particular seventh verse. It is not to be found in any single Greek text of this epistle before the fourteenth century. It was a verse that gradually began to make its appearance in certain Latin versions, and eventually it got into this Greek text, which was first published by Erasmus. Interestingly enough, it was not in his first published text, but objections were made by certain elements of the Roman Church and they said they could produce it in the Greek text from the Latin translation. Now lest you may think I have become a higher critic, let me just say that there is a unanimity about this and a general consensus of opinion that this statement was put in by somebody and has thus found its way into the text and is indeed a spurious statement.

Now at this point I imagine someone saying, 'Surely by saying that, you have undermined my whole confidence in Scripture. If you take that verse out, isn't that equal to the so-called "higher criticism"?' So what is the difference between that which is called textual criticism and what has been given the name of higher criticism? Textual criticism means just this: it is the endeavour of scholars to find out, as far as is possible, the text that approximates most closely to the original document. So it is something in which we should all believe and something that we should encourage. And as you look at these various Greek, Latin, Syrian, Coptic, and Abyssinian texts and so on, you will find a slight variation here and there. But, and this is the point, the variations affect not a single doctrine. They are quite irrelevant. They make no difference to Christian truth; they are more a matter of detail—merely technical. Take, for instance, this particular verse that is verse 7 in the Authorised Version. It makes no difference whatsoever to Christian doctrine if that verse is omitted. The variations are not only slight—they are quite unimportant; and we are entitled to go further and say that the text, so-called, of Westcott and Hort we can undoubtedly take with confidence as being the original manuscripts and documents.

But higher criticism is something very different. The object with which the higher critic sets out is not to find what he can describe as that which approximates clearly to the original. He wants to know certain other things; he want to know what the book contains in a later edition, whether it is a composite work, whether the reputed author is the real author, when the book was first written, and so on. In other words, higher critics approach the Bible as if it were any other book. The man who is concerned about textual criticism starts by saying that it is the inspired Word of God; he is not concerned about pulling it to pieces. But the higher critics begin with certain ideas and propensities, and they make a criticism of this Book in terms of their idea; they place their literary and historical criticism over against the idea of divine inspiration. They do this with regard to the New and the Old Testaments. They say the books of Moses could not possibly have been written by Moses. Deuteronomy, they say, was written not many centuries before Christ came into the world. They say that we know about the history of the world, and they put up their theory of evolution—that men started by worshipping spirits in trees, and since then have gradually evolved from a belief in many gods to a belief in one God. They come to the Scriptures and analyse them in terms of their historical postulate. They believe their so-called historical canon and their literary and scientific canons and therefore they dismiss the miracles; they dismiss the history of the Old Testament, and they likewise dismiss the history of the New Testament.

Now can you see the difference between the two things? Textual criticism leaves the great doctrines exactly where they were; higher criticism is an attack ultimately not only upon the unique inspiration of the Bible but upon the cardinal doctrines and tenets of the Christian faith. It is men setting up their own ideas over and against this revelation. But textual criticism does nothing of the sort. Textual criticism is not concerned to analyse the books of the Bible; it is simply concerned to compare and contrast and collate various documents and manuscripts in order to try to arrive at the right text. It does not start with its ideas and impose this upon the Bible.

I have been led to emphasise all this in order that we may have clearly in our minds this whole question of the statement of the seventh verse. But now, having disposed of that, let us consider the claim that is made here. It is: 'This is he that came by water and blood, even Jesus Christ; not by water only, but by water and blood. And it is the Spirit that beareth witness, because the Spirit is truth. For there are three that bear record . . . the spirit, and the water, and the blood: and these three agree in one.'

Now I think that John means this: he is concerned about the person of the Lord, and he wants to give his readers evidence; he wants to produce witnesses who will not only confirm and substantiate their faith, but will also give them real confidence. The claim is, of course, the claim that he puts into words, and those words are, 'Jesus Christ.' He has already said, 'He that believeth that Jesus is the Son of God'; here he says 'Jesus Christ.' On whom am I going to rely; on whom am I going to rest my faith? And the answer is: Jesus Christ–the God-Man.

In other words, this is another interesting way of stating the doctrine of the incarnation, and that is something which John has been doing from the very beginning. 'That which was from the beginning, which we have heard, which we have seen with our eyes, which we have looked upon, and our hands have handled, of the Word of life'—you remember that he started on that; everything depended upon Jesus Christ, and here he comes back to it again. The whole doctrine rests, in a sense, upon this vital doctrine of the incarnation.

Who is Jesus of Nazareth? And the answer is, He is 'Jesus Christ.' He is Jesus; He is a man; He was born as a baby and laid in a manger. He was a boy, and He argued with the Doctors in the Temple. He worked as a carpenter; He was a man who suffered hunger and thirst. He said that there were certain things He did not know—Jesus. Yes, but 'Jesus Christ'—He is the Anointed of God; He is the Messiah long expected, the one whom God has set apart in order that this mighty work of redemption and salvation might be brought about. It is very difficult, in a sense, to put this because while it is right in a way to say that He is man and He is also God, there is another sense in which one should never say that, because He is only one person—two natures in the one person, and yet only one person. He is not so much man and God—He is God-Man, two in one, not intermingled—'Jesus Christ.'

Now that is the great thing that John is here anxious to assert; we must be perfectly clear in our minds with regard to this person— who He is and therefore what He has done. 'But,' someone may ask, 'if that is what he is concerned about, why does he drag in this idea about coming not by water only but by water and by blood?'

Here again there have been many different views with regard to that. There are those who tell us that this reference to the water and the blood is simply a reminder of what John reports at the end of his Gospel. He tells us about the crucifixion, that when the spear was thrust into Christ's side, there came out blood and water. Obviously, they say, he is just referring back to that. Yet it seems to me that that is quite impossible as an explanation. To start with, John, in the Gospel, refers to 'blood and water'; this is a reference to 'water and blood.' Not only that, but he goes out of his way to say, 'Not by water only, but by water and blood.' In other words, he is not so much referring to blood and water as to water and blood: they are separate, and they are distinct, and they must be held apart. Thus I cannot accept the explanation that this just refers to the blood and water that came from the pierced side of our Lord.

Then there are others who tell us that this has reference to the two sacraments—the sacrament of baptism and the sacrament of the Lord's Supper. Here, again, is something that cannot be made to sit easily upon what we are considering together. John has made no reference to the sacraments; he is, rather, concerned with objective witness to the deity and the uniqueness of the person of our Lord and Saviour Jesus Christ.

So again we must ask the question, what does he mean by saying this? Well, it seems that the best way to approach the subject is to look at it like this: John is concerned to establish the reality of the incarnation, to prove that Jesus Christ is really the Son of God incarnate, in the flesh. I believe that he was anxious to do so in order to correct a heresy that was very prevalent at that time, which we have had occasion to mention previously. It taught, let me remind you, something like this: Jesus of Nazareth was a man, but when He was baptised by John in the Jordan, the eternal Christ came upon Him and entered into Him, so that from the moment of the baptism the eternal Christ was dwelling in the human Jesus. And He continued to do so until just before the crucifixion took place. Then the eternal Christ went back to heaven, and it was only the man Jesus who was crucified.

Now that was a very common heresy in the first centuries, and it is a heresy that has also been prevalent during these past centuries. This whole trouble during the last hundred years or so about the person of Christ has been nothing, in a sense, but a recapitulation of that ancient heresy; it puts a wedge between the man Jesus and the eternal Christ. And here John is concerned to assert this mighty fact, that the baby in the manger is the God-Man, 'Jesus Christ,' and not Jesus only. The incarnation is a reality, and the one who died upon the cross was not only the man Jesus—it was the

God-Man who died. And I believe that John mentions this testimony and witness of the water and the blood in order to establish the unity and the oneness of the person; not two persons, but one person with the two natures.

That, it seems to me, is the main division of these verses, but we shall go on to show how John, in a still more detailed way, maintains that there are these three witnesses to this unique person. We shall see how he demonstrates that the water and the blood, in addition to the Spirit, assert this, and he assures us that the one in whom we repose our faith is none other than the only begotten Son of God.

We must be certain of these things, and it is in order to give us that certainty that the Apostle has thus written.

7

The Three Witnesses

This is he that came by water and blood, even Jesus Christ;
not by water only, but by water and blood. And it is the
Spirit that beareth witness, because the Spirit is truth. For
there are three that bear record in heaven, the Father, the
Word, and the Holy Ghost: and these three are one. And
there are three that bear witness in earth, the spirit, and the
water, and the blood: and these three agree in one.

1 JOHN 5:6-8

In this section (1 John 5:6-12), John is dealing with the great doctrine of belief in Jesus Christ as the Son of God, and we suggested that it could be divided roughly into three divisions: the
claim that is made (vv 6-8); the witness that is borne, and, in verses
9 and 10, the reason we are to accept this witness and this claim;
and in verses 11 and 12, the consequences of believing the testimony. We also indicated that the whole object, generally, is to establish faith and give us certainty—to have this faith in Jesus Christ as
the Son of God, to be certain of Him, and to know exactly in whom
we have this belief. So John takes up this theme of the person of our
Lord, and we saw that, having in mind the heresy that would put
a wedge between Jesus the man and Jesus the eternal Christ, John
is arguing for the unity of the person. Jesus Christ is one person. It

is the Son of God who was born as a baby, and it was the Son of God who died on the cross—not only the man, but the God-Man. But this is not the only object of John's statements. Indeed, I would say that it is not even his main or particular object. I think his main object is to show that Jesus, the Son of God, is the Christ of God, the one who came to do what was so necessary for mankind and its salvation. Indeed, this is the only way in which we can understand these difficult verses. John is concerned particularly here to establish the fact that Jesus is the Christ, the Messiah, the long-expected Saviour, the long-awaited deliverer of His people.

He is stressing this for two main reasons. The first is that we are driven to that conclusion by the changing of the terminology in verses 5 and 6: 'Who is he that overcometh the world, but he that believeth that Jesus is the Son of God?' (v 5); 'This is he that came by water and blood, even Jesus Christ' (v 6). You see, it is no longer Jesus is 'the Son of God,' but Jesus is the 'Christ'; and I suggest that when John varies his expression like that, he has a very deliberate object in mind. He does it not just for the sake of doing so, but because he is bringing out some additional meaning.

There is a second reason for arguing that this is right. It is the very interesting word came—'This is he that came.' It is also a significant word, because 'coming' carries with it not merely the fact that He has come, but the purpose of His coming. We can follow this word as it is used in the Scriptures. Take, for instance, the question set to our Lord by John the Baptist: 'Art thou he that should come?' Now that was a phrase among the Jews; the Messiah was the one who was to come and do certain things.

Take also the statement by John in the first chapter of his Gospel—'For the law was given by Moses, but grace and truth came by Jesus Christ' (1:17). 'Grace and truth came'; He is the one who brought, He is the conveyor of, grace and truth; and there are other instances of the same expression. In other words, John is not only referring to the birth of our Lord Jesus Christ in a literal sense, but also to the coming of the one who has brought and was to bring certain benefits to mankind. He is coming as the Messiah, so that in effect what John is saying is this: 'He is coming to us as a Messiah by water and blood; not with water only, but with blood'; there is the clue to the understanding of these verses that have so often perplexed people.

We have seen that we could not completely understand this as a reference to the blood and water that came from His side when He died. We also indicated that it is surely not right to say that the water and the blood referred to the sacraments of baptism and the Lord's Supper. If you consider the various suggestions that have been made, you will be driven to the conclusion that the references to water and blood are references to the baptism and the death of our Lord. How do we fit these in together? Well, let us look at it like this:

The great business of the Messiah who was to come was to deliver the people from the thraldom and bondage of sin and its consequences. Men and women, as a result of their sin, were under the wrath of God. They needed to be delivered from the power of the world, the flesh, and the devil—the power of sin both inside and outside. So the Messiah, the Saviour, had to make expiation for our sin and set us free from its power. This was His great task. And John tells us that Jesus Christ came as the Messiah and has done that, and we see Him doing it as we look at His baptism and as we see His death on the cross. His baptism, in a sense, is the beginning of His power as the Messiah—He came as the Messiah by 'water.' Through that He identifies Himself with our sin, and it is upon the cross that He deals with it, expiates it, and delivers us from the wrath of God and therefore from the power of sin and the power of the world, the flesh, and the devil.

Now I think we see why John does not refer to Christ's birth in his Gospel. He has been pointing to Christ as the Messiah, fixing his attention upon that, that Jesus is the Son of God. So he does not refer to the birth; but he does refer to the baptism. And so I think we see very clearly why it is that we have the phrase 'not by water only, but by water and blood.' The Lord Jesus Christ did not merely identify Himself with us and our sins–He went further; He dealt with it not in water only, but also in the blood. His death is an absolute essential in addition to the baptism.

That, therefore, I suggest to you, is the statement that John makes. He is not only interested in the person of our Lord, but in the work also. John was never interested in our Lord, if I may so put it, in a mere theoretical manner. He wanted to help these people. He wanted them to know that what our Lord had done applied to their immediate condition and to their immediate need. It is only, therefore, as we say, 'This is our Messiah' that we can be delivered from and overcome the power of the world, the flesh, and the devil and everything that is set against us.

The next phrase is, 'it is the Spirit that beareth witness, because the Spirit is truth.' This is, I think, a reference to the particular testimony that is borne to all of us by the Holy Spirit, a testimony to the saving work of Christ. How does the Holy Spirit do this? John is referring to the descent of the Holy Ghost on the Church on the Day of Pentecost at Jerusalem and the consequences that followed. He is primarily interested in objective witnesses, and so his emphasis is that the Holy Spirit is bearing final testimony to the fact that Jesus is the Christ. John says that the Spirit is the truth. He is the Spirit of God; He is God; and so there is the final proof that Jesus is the deliverer, the Messiah. Let us then examine the details of this extrordinary statement.

The peculiar and special matter with which the Apostle is dealing is this description of our Lord and Saviour as the emancipator, the Saviour who has come to take away the sins of the world; but that leads him to make a further statement. In verse 8 John says, 'And there are three that bear witness in earth, the spirit, and the water, and the blood: and these three agree in one.' The proof is in His suffering. 'This is he that came by water and blood, even Jesus Christ,' and the Spirit bears witness to this, and that makes John think in terms of the witnesses that are borne–'the spirit, and the water, and the blood.'

What does he want to prove by that? What is it that we, as believers, need to know? I think the best way to answer these questions is to remind ourselves of what was after all the essential and characteristic thinking of the Apostles. What exactly was their message? In Acts 17 we read this: 'And Paul, as his manner was, went in unto them, and three sabbath days reasoned with them out of the Scriptures. Opening and alleging, that Christ must needs have suffered, and risen again from the dead; and that this Jesus, whom I [Paul] preach unto you, is Christ' (vv 2-3).

In other words, the Apostles set out to do two things: they had to prove that the long-awaited Messiah must of necessity suffer, that He would be put to death; and the second thing they had to do was to prove that Jesus was the Messiah. So the things we find John emphasising here are the things that Paul emphasised, three things that bear witness–'the spirit, and the water, and the blood.' How do they do so? There are certain headings I will give you that you can work out for yourselves. Take first this witness or testimony. How did the Spirit bear testimony to the fact that Christ was the Son of God, the Messiah?

First, in the baptism you remember that John told the people, 'I knew him not: but he that sent me to baptize with water, the same said unto me, Upon whom thou shalt see the Spirit descending, and remaining on him, the same is he which baptizeth with the Holy Ghost' (John 1:33). He therefore bore witness and testimony to the fact that Christ is the Lamb of God. But not only that; the Holy Spirit also bears witness to Him in His life. Look at the words of our Lord, and look at His works. How can you explain Him? How can you explain these things in Him? There is only one answer. 'God giveth not the Spirit by measure unto him' (John 3:34). He is filled with the Spirit, and thus He is able to speak His words and do His perfect works. Indeed, Paul says that He is 'declared to be the Son of God with power, according to the spirit of holiness, by the resurrection from the dead' (Rom 1:4).

But then the next great way in which the Spirit bears this witness is in what happened on the Day of Pentecost, which shows that Christ is in particular the Messiah in His sending of the gift of the Spirit to the Church.

The Spirit bears this witness in the Church herself and in the testimony of the life of the Church. Peter says to the Jewish rulers, 'And we are his witnesses of these things; and so is also the Holy Ghost, whom God hath given to them that obey him' (Acts 5:32). There is the witness and testimony of the Holy Spirit, and in all these ways he testifies to the fact that Jesus is the Christ.

How next does the water, the baptism, bear witness? Well, we have emphasised the descent of the Holy Ghost upon Christ; there He is, being baptised in the Jordan, and the Spirit in the form of a dove descends upon Him. And we read that a voice spoke from heaven saying, 'This is my beloved Son, in whom I am well pleased' (Matt 3:17). In the baptism God bears witness and testimony to the fact that this is the Christ, this is the Messiah, this is the one who is come to do the work that has been allotted to Him. 'The spirit, and the water'–the testimony of the two are the same and bring us to the same conclusion.

But the last witness is centred on Christ's death on the cross. How does this bear witness? Why is John so anxious to emphasise it? Not the water only, but the blood–how does this prove that Jesus is the Christ and that He must suffer and be slain to save us? In the first place like this: the very fact that the death led to the resurrection is proof that Jesus is the Son of God. It was the resurrection that established it, and the death is the ultimate proof. But that is not the most important. It is as we look at the death that we see He is the Christ and the Saviour. The Jews had a false view of the Messiah. He was to them a man who was to emancipate them politically and militarily. But He did not do this, and so they crucified Him. They jeered at Him and despised Him and said, 'Why not come to Jerusalem and be crowned? If you are the Messiah why not declare yourself?' A Prince? No! That was their error; but 'it behoved Christ to suffer' (Luke 24:46).

That was the preaching of the Apostles, and it was not merely *their* preaching—it was the very thing our Lord Himself had taught. He wanted to show the disciples that all He had done was the work that His Father had sent Him to do. The Old Testament Scriptures show us that everything that happened to Him was a fulfilment of the old prophecies. And when the Apostles preached this, they were after all doing nothing but repeating His own words to them. 'And he said unto them, These are the words which I spake unto you, while I was yet with you, that all things must be fulfilled, which were written in the law of Moses, and in the prophets, and in the psalms, concerning me. Then he opened their understanding, that they might understand the Scriptures, and said unto them, Thus it is written, and thus it behoved Christ to suffer, and to rise from the dead the third day: and that repentance and remission of sins should be preached in his name among all nations, beginning at Jerusalem. And ye are witnesses of these things. And, behold, I send the promise of my Father upon you: but tarry ye in the city of Jerusalem, until ye be endued with power from on high' (Luke 24:44-49).

What does He mean? Again, you see, it is that the Messiah was to suffer. They all said He was to suffer and die. The Messiah, the Christ, was to be the suffering servant, and one on whom the sins of the world are laid and who is punished. 'Don't be depressed by the death on the cross,' he said in effect to his disciples; 'it was only by dying that I could set you at liberty.'

So the death—the blood—is the ultimate establishment of the fact that He is the Christ, the deliverer, the Messiah. He said it, and He proved it, and it was the burden of the apostolic preaching.

So, then, I look at Him dying and ask myself, 'If He is the Son of God, why this?' Because it was the only way in which the Son of God could save us. It was the only way in which the Son of God could emancipate us and set us free. It had to be. I look at Him on the cross, and I listen, and hear Him say, 'It is finished' (John 19:30). What is finished? The work the Father had given Him to do; the work for which He was baptised and the work for which he died; the work for which He became the Messiah. The special work of the Messiah, the Christ, the Saviour, had been fully accomplished. This is the fact to which the three bear witness. That is the fact about which the three agree—that Jesus is the Christ and that Christ must suffer.

What do *we* say about it? As I look and listen to the evidence of the three witnesses I repeat the words of Peter: 'Lord, to whom shall we go? thou hast the words of eternal life. And we believe and are sure that thou art that Christ, the Son of the living God' (John 6:68-69). He is the one who gave Himself to the work of His Father and to the death on the cross. If He had not died, I would not be forgiven, I could not be saved. Jesus is the Son of God. Jesus is the Christ of God.

8

Eternal Life

If we receive the witness of men, the witness of God is greater: for this is the witness of God which he hath testified of his Son. He that believeth on the Son of God hath the witness in himself: he that believeth not God hath made him a liar; because he believeth not the record that God gave of his Son. And this is the record, that God hath given to us eternal life, and this life is in his Son. He that hath the Son hath life; and he that hath not the Son of God hath not life.

1 JOHN 5:9-12

We look once more at these words, in this vitally important and interesting paragraph running from the sixth verse to the end of the twelfth verse. The Apostle is really bringing to a conclusion the subject matter of his letter, and he ends with this great statement concerning the person of our Lord and Saviour Jesus Christ. Now let me remind you, I have suggested that the most convenient way of subdividing this matter is that in verses 6, 7, and 8 he is stating a claim; in 9 and 10 he gives the reasons for believing it; and in 11 and 12 he reminds us of the consequences of belief.

We have already considered verses 6 to 8 and have seen how John shows that the Messiah, long expected, is none other than

Jesus of Nazareth, the Son of God. Now here, in verses 9 and 10, he gives us various reasons for believing that, and we must, therefore, consider them together.

These verses can be subdivided into two divisions, and it might be well to take them together and indicate three reasons why we should accept this testimony concerning Jesus as the Son of God and the Saviour. After all, someone may say, 'You exhort us to believe that Jesus is the Christ and the Son of God. Why should we? On what grounds?'

The first answer is, the nature of the evidence. You may look at this if you like in a different way. In a changing, uncertain world we need something certain; and John wants people to have this certainty. The first element is that there is objective, external evidence provided for us. 'If we receive the witness of men, the witness of God is greater: for this is the witness of God which he hath testified of his Son. He that believeth on the Son of God hath the witness in himself . . .'

John there is surely saying that the witness to which we have been paying attention—namely the Spirit, the water, and the blood—is none other than the testimony of God Himself. This is a matter of which we are quite certain. We have the evidence from the baptism, the evidence of the death on the cross and the Day of Pentecost, and the subsequent evidence of the events of the Church; the three agree in one.

Now, it is the custom of natural man to accept the evidence of two or three witnesses—people and witnesses who can be relied upon. If you have two or three such people bearing the same testimony, you accept them. Therefore, says John, if we accept the witness of man, 'the witness of God is greater.' And this is the witness of God: it was *God* who was testifying in the baptism that Jesus is the Christ. It is God who has provided that evidence. It is God, likewise, who has provided the evidence of the blood in Christ's death on the cross. It is *God* who is doing this, and He further did it by raising Christ from the dead. It is through the resurrection that He has declared Christ to be the Son of God, His Son. And the evidence of the Holy Spirit is the evidence of God because He is God. He is the third person in the Trinity.

So why should I believe on Jesus Christ? Well, if you have no other answer, God has told you that this is the Messiah. It is not merely the testimony of man, but the testimony of God, and over and above all other testimony our case rests on this fact–that this is a revelation from God. This is not a philosophy. This is not something that man thinks. It is not human imagination; it is not a myth. We claim that we have here a revelation from God, and the reason for believing this message is that it is the witness and testimony of God Himself. But John puts it negatively as well as positively: 'He that believeth not God hath made him a liar; because he believeth not the record that God gave of His Son.'

This is a terrifying thought, and I wonder whether we realise it as we should. Not to believe the gospel and the Christian message is to say that God is a liar. Is there anyone uncertain about these things, anyone who talks about difficulties and says, 'My mind is not fully satisfied'? If there is such a person I have great sympathy with you. But I would remind you that this statement comes from *God*; God Himself is giving testimony. But quite apart from your difficulties, so-called, I would remind you that this is a question of accepting testimony and witness. God has said, '*This is my beloved Son*, in whom I am well pleased; hear ye him' (Matt 17:5). Am I to refuse Him? Well, the terrifying thing is that if I do, I am saying that God's pronouncement is not true. That is the position in which it involves us; for here we start on a different level. It is a revelation from God. It is the Almighty Himself who tells us this, and it is not a question of pitting our minds against a human teaching. It is a statement from Heaven, and to reject it is to say that God is a liar.

The second argument is this: in addition to the external evidence there is also the subjective or internal evidence. John puts it in this way: 'He that believeth on the Son of God hath the witness in himself . . .' So we are dealing here with these two different stands–the external and the internal, and this is a very great and important subject. I am not at all sure but that this is not the most vital of all the parts of the subject. It was a great matter to the minds of the Reformers. They clearly defined this matter. The believer is confronted by two great sources of certainty, one outside and one inside–*Spiritus Externus* and *Spiritus Internus*.

But perhaps the best way to understand this is to ask ourselves, 'How may I know that the Bible is the Word of God?' There are two main ways. There is the Word itself–the testimony of the Holy Spirit, and the agreement of the books written within it. This general consensus, the internal unity of the Bible, and various other arguments–this is the *Spiritus Externus*–the outside testimony. But according to the Reformers, that is not enough to give people certainty. They need something inside as well, and the Holy Spirit also gives them that internal certitude–the *Spiritus Internus*. Let me put this personally. There was a time when I read the Bible and thought it was a wonderful book; I felt it was a unique book and that I could not compare it with any other book. But then the time came when I was confronted with the great evidence given to me in the Gospels and the Old and New Testaments, and I had a feeling within me that this was the Word of God. That is what it means–this internal evidence.

Paul, in 1 Corinthians 2, refers to 'the princes of this world' (v 8), these wise men who all looked at Jesus Christ and failed to recognise that He was the Lord of glory. They lacked the Spirit who enables us to understand the great things of God that have been given to us. But 'He that believeth on the Son of God hath the witness in himself,' and it is important that we should bear this in mind–this internal certainty first that Jesus is the Christ, and second that I myself am a child of God.

So am I happy in my Christian life? Do I know in whom I have believed? Am I ready to meet all the contingencies that may come to me? Does a possible war, illness, or trouble distress me? In death, in that unknown future, how do I stand with respect to these things? Now, it is just at this point that this element of certainty comes in. There is all the difference in the world in accepting the Word of God and knowing for certain that these things are true. There have been many who have gone through a lifetime, thinking they have this belief in God and in His Word, living the Christian life; and yet when they came to their deathbeds they felt lonely and deserted. They had no certainty just when they needed it. In other words, I am sure that without this witness in ourselves there is no peace and no real satisfaction. We are provided with everything we need; we are not asked to rest alone on something external. If you believe this, you will have the witness within yourself as well.

Of course, there are certain difficulties to which I must refer. How is this certainty to be obtained? Here is the most important principle, and we must observe the order in which these things come: the objective must come first. We try to have the subjective, but notice the order. First I am to receive the witness of God, and it is only after I have that that I am likely to have the evidence and the witness within myself. There is a statement in Psalm 34 that says, 'Taste and see that the Lord is good' (v 8). The trouble is, we want to see before we have tasted. No! Taste and then you will see that the Lord is good. Or take the way the Lord Himself put it in his teaching. He said, 'If any man will do his [God's] will, he shall know of the doctrine' (John 7:17). So if you want to be certain, believe first, and then you will be certain.

So this question of the order is a vitally important one. Believe God, and then have the belief within yourself. To reverse the order would be insulting to God. Someone may say, 'Well, I will only believe if I have proof.' But God says, 'I ask you to believe because I am speaking'; so not to believe is dishonouring to Him. To try to insist that you must have proof is to detract from His glory. So first I must believe because God is the witness; and if I do, then I shall have the witness of the Spirit within myself.

The other practical thing, of course, is just to learn exactly what believing His evidence means, and here John puts it in a very few words: 'He that believeth on the Son of God hath the witness in himself.' Oh, what important words these are; what an important word is that little word 'on'! John does not mean us to say, 'Well, on the whole I am satisfied with the evidence, and I am prepared to believe that Jesus of Nazareth is the Son of God.' So I put down my book and prepare to argue with my friends and we can all meet and have a discussion. And after a long discussion, we come to the conclusion that we are satisfied that the claim made does really convince us that Jesus is the Son of God.

That is not it! 'He that believeth on the Son of God . . .' Such a person has abandoned himself to Him. He has surrendered to Him. He is the man who says, 'I look on Him, and I see the Saviour, the Son of God, sent by God. I am under the wrath of God. I am a doomed, guilty, foul sinner, and there He is—the one who can deliver me. So I cast myself upon Him, "just as I am without one plea."' You can give your intellectual assent to the truth perhaps sitting comfortably or in a discussion, but you can only believe on the Son of God on your knees. You may not realise the full implications of the statement, but you hand over your whole life into the strong arms of the Son of God. And you will very soon have the witness. You will know who He is, and all your uncertainties will have gone. Jesus is not only the Christ, He is the Son of God, the Messiah, the deliverer of the world.

And that brings us to the last great argument, in verses 11 and 12, which is that we are to believe it because of the consequences that follow. It is not only that we are to be certain of eternal life. 'God hath given to us eternal life, and this life is in His Son. He that hath the Son hath life; and he that hath not the Son of God hath not life.' We are considering all this because our eternal future depends on these things. We either have life or we are dead, and to come out of this world spiritually dead means to go out to the wrath of God, to go out into an eternity of darkness and death.

Our Lord has said, 'This is life eternal, that they might know

thee the only true God, and Jesus Christ, whom thou hast sent'
(John 17:3). Do you know God? I do not ask you if you say your
prayers. Do you know that He has loved you with an everlasting
love? Do you know that He is yours? Can you say, '*My* God'? Do
you know He is your Father? If you know Christ, you know God,
for you know Jesus whom He has sent. You are full of a new life.
'Christ liveth in me.' Can you say that?

To be a Christian is not merely to hold certain Christian
philosophies. It is more than that. You are able to say, 'I am a new
man or woman. I am not what I was. I, yet not I. God is dwelling
in me.' And John emphasises this. Why is it so important that I
should be clear about Jesus Christ? Why is it I should be certain
He is the Son of God, the Christ, the Messiah? 'This is the record,
that God hath given to us eternal life, and this life is in his Son.' If
you have not the Son, you have not life. 'This is my beloved Son,
in whom I am well pleased,' God said at His baptism. He has put
it all into Him. Life is entirely, exclusively, solely in the Son of God,
so that if I am not clear about these facts—that Jesus is the Son of
God, and that Jesus is the Christ—then I have not life. Eternal life
is only available as I believe—if I go to Jesus Christ for it. So unless
I can say, 'and of his fulness have [I] received, and grace for [or
upon] grace' (John 1:16), I am without life, I am dead. In other
words, it is not my belief alone that saves me. I have received the
gift of life, and I can face death and judgment with this evidence
that I am a child of God, because in Jesus Christ I have received
eternal life, the life of God Himself, in my own soul.

9

Certain Knowledge

These things have I written unto you that believe on the name of the Son of God; that ye may know that ye have eternal life, and that ye may believe on the name of the Son of God.

1 JOHN 5:13

It is generally agreed that the right translation of this verse is more like this: 'These things have I written unto you, that you may know you have eternal life, that believe on the name of the Son of God.' The meaning is exactly the same in both cases, because those who do believe on the name of the Son of God may *know* that they have eternal life.

This obviously is a very important verse, perhaps the most important in the entire epistle, for in it the Apostle is looking back. He has finished his letter, and here he looks back and summarises what he has been saying and reminds the people of his object when he began to write.

He has said that he was anxious that they might have fellowship with him and with the other Apostles, because the fellowship was with the Father and with his Son Jesus Christ. John was particularly anxious that these people to whom he had been writing should be clear as to the central purpose of his letter. That is something that is very necessary, because our danger is to miss the forest because of the trees. It is absolutely necessary to be clear about everything, but we must also bear in mind the purpose of it all; and the Apostle reminds us of his ultimate object, which is that those who are Christians, those who believe on the name of the Son of God, might know that they have eternal life. 'These things have I written unto you . . . that ye may *know* . . .'

Now there can be no question that this is the most important statement that could ever be made to a company of men and women. In John 17 this is emphasised from beginning to end. There was our Lord, immediately prior to His death on the cross, reviewing His life and praying not concerning the world, but concerning those whom God had given Him, and He says exactly the same thing. His prayer was that men and women might know God and Jesus Christ whom He had sent. He had come to bring eternal life, and in that prayer He goes on repeating His desire that the men and women whom God had given Him might possess this full knowledge and glory in it.

We have been repeating that as we have worked our way through this epistle. This is the essence of the Christian life, that we might have the full knowledge of God and that we may know we have it. In the immediate context we see that John has been emphasising and stressing a prior knowledge—that Jesus of Nazareth is really the Son of God and the Messiah. He wants the people to know for certain the truth concerning Him—that they might know for certain that they possess eternal life and the full knowledge of God. So it is important for us to understand exactly what the Apostle is telling us here, and we can look at it in a number of propositions.

This knowledge that we have eternal life is something that is possible to us. That is something that needs to be emphasised. There are those who would tell us that eternal life is something to which we attain only when we come to die and leave this world and go into the next. They suggest that it is wrong for anyone to claim that he *has* eternal life. Such people dislike the doctrine of assurance. 'We do not know,' they say, 'and we must not seek to know. Faith means that you are always grasping at it, but it is something you cannot actually have while you are in this world.'

But that is a philosophical concept of faith that is not in accordance with what we have here. John says, 'My whole object in writing to you now is that you may know you have eternal life and know it certainly. I want you to *know* that you possess it.' You find the other Apostles saying the same thing. What was more characteristic of the Apostle Paul than this assurance? In Romans 8 he says, 'For I am persuaded, that neither death, nor life, nor angels, nor principalities, nor powers, nor things present, nor things to come, nor height, nor depth, nor any other creature, shall be able to separate us from the love of God, which is in Christ Jesus our Lord' (vv 38-39). 'I know whom I have believed,' he writes to Timothy (2 Tim 1:12). 'I *know*,' he says. There is no uncertainty about it.

So it seems to me that to interpret faith as a kind of constant uncertainty is to deny the teaching of the Word of God that we are His children. Indeed, 'the Spirit itself beareth witness with our spirit, that we are the children of God' (Rom 8:16). Such knowledge is possible to us. We ought to be in a position of knowing that we have eternal life, that we know God, and that we know Christ.

The second proposition is that this is not only possible, but it is possible to all of us. I have often met people who have taken up a position like this: they say that there are some special men and women who do have this certain knowledge. Yes, John wished everybody to have it, but, of course, he was in that position. So was Peter. They were unique men; they were apart. The spiritual can attain to this knowledge, but it is not meant for us all.

But the answer to that is to repeat the Scripture. There is no such distinction drawn in the New Testament. John is desirous that all these people to whom he writes may share the knowledge that has been given to him. 'That which we have seen and heard,' he says at the beginning of his letter, 'declare we unto you, that ye also may have fellowship with us: and truly our fellowship is with the Father, and with his Son Jesus Christ' (1:3). And here he puts it quite as strongly: 'These things have I written unto you that believe on the name of the Son of God; that ye may know . . .'

In the same way the Apostle Peter, writing to the early Christians, said that they obtained 'like precious faith with us' (2 Pet 1:1)–that is, not a lesser faith, but the same faith. And precisely the same is taught in all the epistles of the Apostle Paul. Yet the Roman Catholic teaching has always divided people into two groups–those who are saints and those who are not. But we are all called to be 'saints' according to the New Testament, and I sometimes think that we rob ourselves of some of the most glorious blessings the New Testament has to offer. There is no such thing as an 'ordinary Christian.' There is a division of labour, but here we are dealing with basic Christian experience. Every Christian is meant to have this certain knowledge of eternal life, this immediate fellowship and communion with God. It is possible for all.

Then the third step is this: it is the duty of all to possess it, and I argue that in this way: it is obvious that God means us to have it. Our Lord Himself says that is why He came into the world. The work that He has now finished is to enable us to have eternal life, to make it possible for us to enter into this blessed and amazing knowledge of God. And, therefore, I argue that it is dishonouring to God for us not to possess it. Indeed, it can be said that we have no right *not* to have this knowledge.

But an argument put forward by people who say that they would not like to presume that they have salvation or that they know they have eternal life is that such a statement makes us Pharisees and makes us say, 'Thank God we are not as other men.' Yet it should not do so, because eternal life is something that we receive from God as a gift. He has offered it to us, and He sent His Son to a cruel death on the cross that we might receive it. So I repeat, we have no right not to have it. If Christian people are uncertain as to the fact that they have eternal life, they are dishonouring God, and they are bearing a very poor witness and testimony to the power of salvation.

Then let me come to a more practical and personal reason why we should have it. It is that if I am uncertain of my position and of salvation, I shall probably spend most of my time putting myself right. How can the blind lead the blind? My first business is to get right myself. In my reading of Scripture and in meditation I then shall have to be centring on myself. I am lacking in power and witness and effective testimony. The only way to be strong is to be certain about all this, and the history of the Church bears out that statement abundantly.

Read the stories of the martyrs and confessors; read the stories of those men and women who gave their lives for their beliefs, those who went to the stake and died for the truth. What was their secret? What made them so strong? The answer is that these men and women *knew* in whom they believed. They possessed eternal life, and the only effect of the death at the stake was to usher them into salvation and to bring them face to face with their Lord Jesus Christ. If they had been uncertain of all this, they could not have faced such a trial.

It is equally essential now. You cannot really know the joy of the Lord until you are perfectly certain that all is well between you and God. And the way to have this joy is to have this eternal life, which means fellowship with God and with His Son, Jesus Christ. This knowledge is possible, and possible for all; and it is our duty to have the knowledge before we take any other step. Therefore, let me ask you another simple question: do you know that you have eternal life; have you this knowledge? This is what is offered. This is what we are meant to have. It is this that makes a brighter and more confident testimony. Can we say, 'I know that I have eternal life'?

So let us do what John invites us to do. Let us remind ourselves of the way in which we can have this certain knowledge that we do really possess eternal life. John has gone on repeating it, and I have reminded you of it, but let us say it all once more. How do I know I have this?

Before I touch on any difficulties there are certain tests by which, if we apply them to ourselves, we may know that we have this knowledge of God. The first is our belief concerning the Lord Jesus Christ Himself. John started and ended with this: 'That which was from the beginning, which we have heard, which we have seen with our eyes, which we have looked upon, and our hands have handled, of the Word of life; (For the life was manifested, and we have seen it, and bear witness, and shew unto you that eternal life, which was with the Father, and was manifested unto us).' That is how he began the letter. He was referring to the Lord Jesus Christ, and in this chapter he says, 'He that hath the Son hath life; and he that hath not the Son of God hath not life.'

In other words, this is something basic; we need not consider any other question if we are not right about this. The first question I must answer is: what is Jesus Christ to me? What do I think of Him? What is my view of this person, Jesus of Nazareth, the one of whom we read in the pages of the four Gospels? The whole point of this is to show that if I have any uncertainty about Him, I have no eternal life. There is no such thing as a knowledge of God apart from Jesus Christ; we never arrive at God truly unless we come through Him.

Therefore, Jesus Christ is absolutely essential to me. He is essential in my scheme and outlook. I have come to see my own unworthiness, my sinfulness, and my smallness. I have seen it deeply and can do nothing to save myself. But God has sent His only begotten Son into the world to do what I cannot do myself. How can I face God? I have but one hope, and that is that God sent His Son. He satisfied God and gave His whole life absolutely, perfectly; He has dealt with the problem of sin. Here is one who has taken my very sins and died for them on the cross, and in Him God forgives me. That is the first essential of this sure knowledge that I have eternal life. Unless I am resting my faith solely in Jesus Christ and His perfect work, I have no life, because the only way to God is in Him.

This leads me to the second test. If I believe all that, I must of necessity come to love God. As I look at Jesus Christ, I see there is only one explanation of this. Jesus Christ is the Son of God, and He has eternal life. 'In this was manifested the love of God toward us, because that God sent his only begotten Son into the world, that we might live through him. . . . We love him, because he first loved us' (1 John 4:9, 19). So this is my second test: what is my attitude towards God? Is He a hard taskmaster? Let me ask myself this question: do I harbour harsh thoughts of God? Do I say when things go wrong, 'God is against me'? But if I believe in the love of Jesus Christ, I believe that God sent Him. So I believe on Him and in the love of God.

But, also, John is very fond of putting this in terms of our attitude towards the world in which we live. 'Love not the world, neither the things that are in the world. If any man love the world, the love of the Father is not in him. For all that is in the world, the lust of the flesh, and the lust of the eyes, and the pride of life, is not of the Father, but is of the world. And the world passeth away, and the lust thereof: but he that doeth the will of God abideth for ever' (1 John 2:15-17).

What is my view of the world when I know for certain that I have eternal life? What is my attitude to the world in which we are all living, the world as we see it in the newspapers—is that what interests me? What am I anxious to obtain? Or am I more interested in these other things—these spiritual things? According to John, Christians are men and women who have come to view the world in an entirely new manner. They see that it is governed by sin. They have come to regard it as a place in which evil forces are at work and whose whole mind is but the working of the spirit of the world. They know that it is something they have to fight, something to withstand, and they realise that unless they do so they will be defeated by it.

Do I hate the world? A good way of answering is this: the Apostle Paul, looking at his surroundings, said, 'For which cause we faint not; but though our outward man perish, yet the inward man is renewed day by day. For our light affliction, which is but for a moment, worketh for us a far more exceeding and eternal weight of glory; while we look not at the things which are seen, but at the things which are not seen; for the things which are seen are temporal; but the things which are not seen are eternal' (2 Cor 4:16-18). In looking at 'the things which are seen,' how much time do I spend in thinking about the Lord God? How much do I think about the glory which is with Him? Which do I meditate upon most—the eternal or the world?

John goes further and says that people who are truly Christians are those who overcome the world. They rise above it; they conquer it. They are in the world, but no longer of it. They are in it, but above it. They may fall into sin, but they do not dally in it; they do not gloat over it. They have been delivered out of this evil world, having been translated out of the kingdom of darkness into the Kingdom of God's dear Son. So what do I really want? Do I want to cling to this world, or do I want to know God whatever it may cost me? Can I answer these questions honestly? Those who have eternal life want more of it.

Then, thirdly, as we have seen, John constantly keeps before us the importance of keeping God's commandments, those commandments which are 'not grievous.' And, finally, we come to the last great test, which is the test of loving the brethren. John says repeatedly that men and women who are Christians will recognise other Christians; they will love them, they will realise that they belong with them, and they will realise that essential unity with them of which our Lord spoke in that great prayer in John 17. Here, then, is a very great test: do we love the brethren? I have sometimes put it like this: if I had the choice of spending an afternoon with a humble saint or with some great earthly personage, which would I choose? Do I want to be where God's people are gathered together? Is that the kind of society that I desire, or is it the other society with all its show and pomp? Love of the brethren is crucial! These tests are very searching, and if we honestly apply them to ourselves we will know where we stand.

Your eternal future depends on this. You have eternal life in this world. It is received here. If you have it, you are destined for glory; but if you die without it, you are destined for perdition. Have you got this life? What is Jesus Christ to you? What is God to you? Do you want to be righteous and holy? Do you want to be like Christ, and do you love the brethren? These are the tests. Our Lord said, '... that they may know thee the only true God, and Jesus Christ, whom thou hast sent' (John 17:3). I am not asking what you believe about God. I am asking, do you *know* Him? Do you believe Him to be your Father? Can you say honestly, 'The Lord is my shepherd, I shall not want' (Psa 23:1). Can you say, '*My* God'? Is He yours? Can you say, 'My Jesus, I love Thee, I know Thou art mine'? Do you know in whom you have believed? Have you received this divine gift?

If you have, God bless you, and may you have it more and more. If you feel honestly that you cannot say that, then what you have to do is very simple. Tell God that you are not certain, that you do not know, and that you desire that knowledge above all else. And ask Him, by His Holy Spirit, to enable you to see your true helplessness, and ask Him to give you the gift. I assure you that if you do, He will not reject you, because He has said, 'Him that cometh to me I will in no wise cast out' (John 6:37). If you have not possessed this, ask Him, believing His own promise, and I assure you that He will answer your prayer. He will give you the gift, and you will *know* you have eternal life.

10

The Life of God

These things have I written unto you that believe on the
name of the Son of God; that ye may know that ye have
eternal life, and that ye may believe on the name of the Son
of God.

1 John 5:13

I come again to this verse because it does seem to me that it is
such a vitally important one that we must try to gain the full
benefit we were intended to gain from it. We have looked at it
in general, from the merely mechanical standpoint, a kind of sum-
mary in and of itself of the entire teaching of the Apostle. We have
reminded ourselves that John here is saying, "That is why I have
written the letter, in order that you might have this certain knowledge that you possess eternal life'; and we have considered John's
own particular tests and applied them to ourselves in order to make
sure that we really do possess this eternal life about which he is
writing.

Now I repeat, this matter is of vital importance. Indeed, it
would not be an exaggeration to say that it is the great theme, the
greatest theme even, in the New Testament itself. It is the whole
object of the New Testament, and it is extraordinary, is it not, how
constantly we seem to forget that. We are interested in forgiveness,

we want to know that our sins are forgiven and that we do not go on to punishment and perdition, and we are interested in living a good life. But for some remarkable reason we tend to persist in forgetting that the ultimate thing that is offered us in the New Testament is nothing less than this very quality of eternal life. The New Testament is really a book that is, in a sense, just meant to tell us that this is what God offers us in Jesus Christ. Is not that the real object that every part of the New Testament has in view?

Why, for instance, do you think that the four Gospels were ever written? Why did the early church not just go on preaching the message of salvation and leave it at that? Now, there can be only one real answer to that question, and it was the answer given by John towards the end of his own Gospel. Having written it, he sums it up like this: 'And many other signs truly did Jesus in the presence of his disciples, which are not written in this book: but these are written, that ye might believe that Jesus is the Christ, the Son of God; and that believing ye might have life through his name' (John 20:30-31). That was why John wrote his Gospel; he was led by the Holy Spirit to do so for that reason.

And what is true of John is equally true of the writers of the other three Gospels. They wrote them not only to give a portrait of the Lord Jesus Christ, but also in order to give this proof and demonstration that Jesus of Nazareth is none other than the Son of God and is indeed the Christ of God, the Messiah, the one who has come into the world bringing life to men and women. You find this as a theme running right through the Gospels. Take that great word which our Lord said to the people: 'I am come that they might have life, and that they might have it more abundantly' (John 10:10); nothing less than that. So we must be clear about the fact that He is the Son of God and that He is the one who brings life.

In the same way the book of Acts is designed to do the same thing. It has that great evidence about His ascension and about the sending of the Holy Spirit on the early church. That is the final proof, as we have already seen, of the fact that He is the Son of God,

the Messiah, the promise of the Father about which the Old
Testament speaks so much. At last the promise has come to us, and
this is the promise of the Holy Spirit, that by Him and through Him
we receive this eternal life. And all the records that you have in the
Acts of the Apostles are nothing but an elaboration of that one
theme. Those first preachers went around saying that they were witnesses of these things; they said, 'We heard His preaching, we saw
His crucifixion, we saw Him buried, we saw the stone rolled over
the mouth of the grave. But we saw Him risen again, we saw the
empty grave, we saw Him ascend, and we received this gift of the
Holy Spirit.' That is the testimony!

The Apostle Paul was as 'one born out of due time' (1 Cor
15:8). He had not been one of the disciples; he had not heard
Christ's teaching in that sense. But he was given a special sight of
the risen Lord in order that he might bear his witness to the fact
that Jesus is the Christ, the Son of God, the one, therefore, who
gives more abundant life to mankind. Furthermore, as I am never
tired of pointing out, that is the great object that lies behind the writers of the New Testament epistles. These letters were written to people who had already believed the gospel. They were written to
churches; they were not open letters to the world, but particular letters to groups of Christian people or to individual Christian believers. But why were they written? They were written because all
these Christians lived in a difficult and gainsaying world. They had
their difficulties; they were tempted perhaps at times to doubt; they
were sometimes defeated by Satan and were falling into temptation.
Various things were going wrong in various ways, and the letters
were written to them in order that they might be strengthened and
encouraged and helped to go forward on their journey.

And the great message to all of them is just this self-same message, that everything they need is in the Lord Jesus Christ; that they
have but to realise that it is His life that they need and that without
it they can do nothing. So the argument of the New Testament from
beginning to end is just that Christ Jesus, the Son of God, came into

the world to give us this eternal life, and this is the most momen-
tous and the most important thing that has ever come to mankind.
In other words, we must once and for ever get rid of this idea
that the New Testament is but a book that contains an exalted teaching that we are meant to practise and to put into action. Not at all!
It is not an exhortation to us to rise to the level of some wonderful
teaching; it is an announcement, it is a proclamation! It calls itself
'good news,' and the amazing good news is that God is giving this
gift of eternal life to all those who have realised their need of it and
are ready to receive it. That is the whole argument, and it is one
that is based very solidly upon facts. So the Gospels and all the
details were written in order to demonstrate to us that this is not
some wonderful idea, some great dream, or some sublime thought.
No; this is something concrete: a person has appeared in this world
who is, in and of Himself, the bearer of this eternal life that God is
giving to mankind. So the one thing to be certain about is that we
know Him.

In a sense, therefore, the New Testament says that the greatest
tragedy that can ever happen is that anyone should be uncertain
about this, that anyone should go on still searching or hoping or
saying, 'Of course I am not to have that while I am in this life and
world; perhaps after death . . . ?' 'Not at all!' says John; 'these things
I have written unto you that believe on the name of the Son of God,
that ye may know that ye have eternal life'—now, not at some future
time.

Now, I put it like that in order that I may lead up to this question: why is it that there is anyone who is at all in difficulty about
this subject? We have looked at some of what I would call the
purely theological reasons. Some people, because of their view of
faith, seem to think that this is impossible, and we showed how that
contradicted the New Testament teaching. But I want now to give
some more practical difficulties that I often find mentioned when
people discuss this together. There are those who seem to be in
trouble about this matter and uncertain as to whether they have

eternal life or not, because they will persist in thinking of it in terms of experience, or in terms of feeling, rather than in the terms that are indicated here. That very often happens in this way. There is always this fatal tendency to standardise the experience of certain notable or outstanding incidents and illustrations.

This is something, I suppose, that is more or less inevitable. There is a tendency in mankind to pay great attention to and to concentrate upon the unusual and the spectacular. We seem to do that instinctively; I suppose it is one of the results of the Fall. Anything unusual or exceptional always attracts attention much more than the usual and the ordinary; that is why some sort of calamity or extraordinary thing in nature always attracts and interests us much more than the perpetual and wonderful things of nature from day to day. Wordsworth discovered that when he said about himself at the end of his great Ode:

> *To me the meanest flower that blows can give*
> *Thoughts that do often lie too deep for tears.*

That is right, and we ought all to put it like that. But the trouble with most of us is that because it is always there we do not marvel at it; that little flower in the hedgerow does not give rise in us thoughts that 'lie too deep for tears.' But if we see a tree struck by lightning we are interested because it is unusual, because it is exceptional.

Now, we tend to do that self-same thing in the whole matter of Christian experience. I attribute this to the Fall, and, of course, one must point out in passing that this is something that tends to be organised and often becomes a business. Those who produce books know that the spectacular always appeals to the mind; so they pick out these exceptional cases and give them great publicity. So we ordinary people who read about them say, 'That is marvellous. If only that had happened to me, then I should know that I have eternal life.' But it has not, and therefore the query arises in my mind as to whether I have eternal life or not. This is the tendency to think of it in terms of experience or feeling, something that comes to us suddenly. I may have gone on for months and years living at a certain level, and suddenly I get some thrilling experience, and I know that from then on all is well. Thus we tend to say that is the only way in which this certainty is to be obtained, and we may well spend a lifetime in waiting for the unusual and the spectacular.

But all that, of course, is just to contradict the essential New Testament teaching. The New Testament never lays stress upon the way in which this comes to us; what it is interested in is the fact that it *has* come. How often, in dealing with enquirers after salvation, does one have to point out that the New Testament never says, 'Whosoever feeleth shall be saved,' but 'whosoever believeth.' People often say, 'In a sense I do accept that teaching; but, you know, I cannot say that I have felt anything.' To which the simple reply is that the New Testament does not insist upon feeling. It says, do you believe; are you prepared to venture your all upon this? So it is sufficient for you to say, 'I live by this; whether I feel or whether I do not does not matter; we are not saved by feeling but by believing.'

And it is exactly the same in this matter of assurance, with this question of knowing that we have eternal life. Let me use an illustration that I once heard an old preacher use. He pointed out that two men may arrive at the end of a journey with their clothes wet all through. But if you enquired as to how it happened to the two men, you might find that it happened in a different way in each case. One man might say that he set out on the journey with the sun shining brilliantly. He had not brought an umbrella or a macintosh as there was no suggestion it was going to rain; but halfway along the road, suddenly the clouds gathered and a veritable downpour took place, and in a moment he was soaked through. The other man's story is a very different one. There was a kind of drizzle all the way through the journey, so he could not tell you when he got wet. The first man could, and the second man could not, but what really matters is not *how* the two men got wet, but the fact that they *are* both wet all through. Whether it happened suddenly or imperceptibly is utterly irrelevant.

So, the vital question is not whether I can point to some vital experience in my life in which I was given certain assurance. The vital question for me is this: as I face these tests in this first epistle of John, do I know that I have life? Whether I have the same experience as somebody else or not, as I examine the tests of life that are given can I say that in spite of my not having had that climactic experience or that thrilling feeling I must have life or I could not say yes to these questions?

Now thinking of it in terms of experience and feeling is a very common cause of trouble. God grant, if there is anyone who has been held in bondage by that kind of difficulty, that they may see the folly of it and may see that what matters, if I may so put it, is not precisely how and when we were born, but the fact that we are alive!

But the second difficulty is this: there are those who feel that before they can say they have eternal life, they ought to be perfect and sinless. They say, 'It is a very great thing to claim that I know I have eternal life, but surely before I can claim that, I ought to be in a position to say that there is no sin and no failure in my life. After all,' they say, 'eternal life is a very wonderful thing, but I cannot say I have it. I am conscious of the fact that I fall and fail and sin; and surely while I am in that condition I cannot make the claim that I have it.' That view, again, is very common.

The simple reply is that John has already dealt with that in the first chapters of this very epistle where he has gone out of his way to say, 'If we say that we have no sin, we deceive ourselves, and the truth is not in us. If we confess our sins, he is faithful and just to forgive us our sins, and to cleanse us from all unrighteousness. If we say that we have not sinned, we make him a liar, and his word is not in us' (1:8-10). The whole of the New Testament, in a sense, is constantly repeating this self-same argument. I wonder whether I can help with regard to this particular difficulty by putting it like this: not only does the New Testament not tell us that we must be able to claim sinless perfection before we can claim we are the possessors of eternal life, but I go so far as to assert that the New Testament itself teaches us quite plainly and clearly that the fact that there is a real struggle in our lives is proof in and of itself of life. 'For the flesh lusteth against the Spirit, and the Spirit against the flesh: and these are contrary the one to the other; so that ye cannot do the things that ye would' (Gal 5:17).

Now, I know that this is teaching that we may wrest to our own confusion, but it is New Testament teaching, and there is a sense in which all New Testament teaching is dangerous. I mean that its teaching is so deep that if we want to misuse it we can do so; hence you have antinomianism. So it means this: before we receive the gift of eternal life, we are dead in trespasses and in sin. There is a stage in which we are at peace; there is no struggle. Of course, we may have heard the moral teaching that is glibly applied by the world, and in our own way we may be concerned and may be striving to reach up to a certain level. But that is not the struggle the New Testament speaks of. The New Testament says that when we receive the gift of eternal life, a new man comes into us, so that we are now two men, and the two are different and contrary—the spirit and the flesh—and there is a struggle and a conflict.

Now those who are aware of that, who though they sin and fail are aware of the fact that there are these two men in them, that there is a struggle between the two—these people have given proof positive that they have received the gift of eternal life. There is no spiritual struggle in the life of unbelievers. There may be a moral struggle, there may be a struggle to live up to a certain code that they have set up, they may struggle to do certain things and if they do not achieve them they are ashamed of themselves—but I am not referring to that. I am referring to a spiritual struggle, to those who are aware of a conflict between two essential things, the one of God and the other of themselves. So you must not allow the devil to depress and discourage you because you occasionally fall into sin or because you say, 'I am not satisfied with my achievements.' If there is this struggle in a spiritual sense, then, according to the New Testament, that of itself is proof that you have eternal life.

Or, to put it slightly differently, there are many who do not say that we must be sinless and perfect before we can make this claim, but after reading the lives of some of the outstanding saints they look at themselves and say, 'Can I claim that I have eternal life when I look at that man or woman?' You must have had that experience; after, for example, reading the life of a man like Hudson Taylor[1] you may have felt you were never a Christian at all. If you have not, there is something wrong with you, for I would regard that as the normal reaction of any Christian. You contrast yourself and you say, 'How can I say I have eternal life when I see such a difference between that man and myself?' and the devil would have us believe that we have no life at all.

Well, again, if we believe that, we are just flying in the face of plain, clear New Testament teaching. The Scripture tells us that we are born into this Christian life as babes, babes in Christ. John in this epistle has been writing to 'little children,' 'young men and old men'; he has a classification and a division (see the second chapter). All that development is possible in this life, so that I think we can answer this particular difficulty by saying, and thank God for this, that a little life is nevertheless life. The baby that was born an hour ago is as much alive as I am; the fact that he is a baby does not mean he is not alive. He is not full-grown, he is not developed, he cannot think and reason, he cannot speak and express himself, but he has life. The babe is as much alive as the old man, and that is the New Testament teaching. So do not let the devil discourage you and rob you in that way; if you are alive at all, you have life.

One of the most gracious words, I think, in the Gospels is that precious word spoken by our Lord where he quotes Isaiah and says, 'The smoking flax he will not quench.' When you look at that flax you may wonder whether there is any fire there at all; it seems absolutely lifeless. But it is all right—there is fire, there is something there; and the smoking flax He will not quench. He will, rather, fan it until it becomes a flame. Though you may have but little life, hold on to the fact that you have life, and thank God for it.

But to sum it all up, we fail to remember that this thing is life, and life is something that shows itself in different ways. Life does not only show itself in feeling and experience—it does so in performing some of the most ordinary common tasks in life; and that is a true test to apply to one's profession of faith. If I have this manifestation of life that John has indicated, I am not interested in feelings, I am not interested in other people's experiences. I face the tests of life, and I see that these things are in me; therefore I must be alive, for a dead man cannot do things like that and would not be like that.

So I would put it in a practical form at this low level. If you are concerned about this question of eternal life, if you feel you have not got it and if it is your greatest ambition to know that you have got it, then you may know that you have got it or you would not have this desire. If you feel that you are empty, if you feel you are nothing, if you feel you are poor and wretched and blind, if you hate your inclination to sin and have any suspicion of a feeling of self-loathing and hatred, you can take it from me that you have eternal life, for no one ever experiences such things until the life of God comes into his or her soul.

There are some further reasons why we should make sure that we have this eternal life. If only we realised the value of this, we would not rest for a moment until we were absolutely certain. Here are some of the reasons: the life that is offered us is nothing less than the life of Jesus Christ; the life you see in Him is the life that He offers. 'I am come,' he says, 'that they might have life, and that they might have it more abundantly' (John 10:10). It is His own life; He gives Himself for the life of the world. We must eat of His flesh and drink of His blood; that means we partake of Him, not the sacrament—we take of *Him*. 'The words that I speak unto you, they are spirit, and they are life,' He says (John 6:63).

In other words, the life that is offered us is the life of God Himself. What an amazing, what a wondrous thought! Yes, but let me go further and say that this life that is offered us is an everlasting life. I know we are often told that eternal life means a quality of life, but it also means duration, and thank God that it does. 'Eternal' includes everlasting, and that means that it is a life that, once I have it, can never be taken away from me. Read the tenth chapter of John. If God gives me His life, and if His life enters into my life, if I am born again of that divine seed, that is an action that is irreversible. Our Lord says of His sheep, 'My Father, which gave them me, is greater than all; and no man is able to pluck them out of my Father's hand' (John 10:29). To me, that is one of the most glorious and amazing things we can ever know, that already there is started in us here something that will go on for ever and ever.

Paul says the same thing, in Romans 8:38-39: 'I am persuaded, that neither death, nor life . . . shall be able to separate us from the love of God, which is in Christ Jesus our Lord.' This is something no one can rob us of, so that whatever may happen to us in this life and world, we have this grand and glorious security. We may be tried and tested and feel ourselves shaking and almost going under, but we have this eternal guarantee behind us.

> *The work which His goodness began*
> *The arm of His strength will complete,*
> *His promise is yea and amen*
> *And never was forfeited yet.*
>
> Augustus Toplady

This is a life that will go on to all eternity; so what we are offered here is a foretaste—these are New Testament terms. We taste the first fruits, so that here on earth, according to this promise, I can begin the great feast that will keep me through the countless ages of all eternity. What a wonderful truth, that here in this world of time I can already sit at the banqueting table and begin to partake and go on without end.

But let me remind you again of what this means. To have eternal life means, as John has reminded us in the third chapter, that I shall see God. If I have this life, I shall see Him; I shall see Christ as He is, and I shall stand in His presence. It is only those who have His nature and share His life and who have been born again who will go on to that; and those who have it will see Him and will be like Him, and they will spend their eternity in glory with Him, enjoying it in His glorious presence.

I remind you of these things, my friends, in order that I may urge anyone who is uncertain to make certain. Would you not like to know you are destined for these things; would you not like to enjoy them here and now? 'That is what is offered,' says John, 'that you may know it now and not lose a second.' But it also helps us in a very practical sense in that if I know I have eternal life already, then I know there is a great life principle working in me. 'Work out your own salvation,' says Paul, 'with fear and trembling: for it is God which worketh in you . . .' And if He is in me in this life, He is working in me 'to will and to do of his good pleasure' (Phil 2:12-13). He is sanctifying me; He is getting things out of my life because He has destined me for that glory; and having destined me for that glory, He will fit me for it.

I have the assurance, therefore, that if this work has begun, the work will end. I 'know' that if I have eternal life, I shall stand one day faultless and blameless, without spot and blemish, in the presence of God's glory. So as I meet temptation and sin in this world, I realise that I am not left to myself. I cease to feel helpless and frustrated. I say, 'If God is in me, if God has destined me for that, then He will come and hold me though all hell and the devils be opposed to me.' That was the mighty argument of a man like Martin Luther. It was because he knew he had eternal life that he could defy all those enemies the way he did, and all those who have this hope in them can say the same thing.

> *And were this world all devils o'er*
> *And watching to devour us,*
> *We lay it not to heart so sore;*
> *Nor they can overpower us.*

If we have eternal life and know that we have it, we know that God's work in our souls will be carried on until it eventuates in that ultimate perfection and glory. As Paul puts it in that mighty bit of logic in the middle of the eighth chapter of Romans, 'Whom he called, them he also justified; and whom'—you see the jump—'he justified, them he also glorified.' If He starts, He will finish, so that if the life is in me, I can be certain of the glory. Far from presuming on that in order to sin, while I am in this life and world I rather say with John, 'Every man that hath this hope in him purifieth himself, even as he is pure' (1 John 3:3). God grant that having listened to these great inducements we all may know for certain that we have eternal life, the life of God in our souls.

11

Prayer with Confidence

And this is the confidence that we have in him, that, if we ask any thing according to his will, he heareth us: And if we know that he hear us, whatsoever we ask, we know that we have the petitions that we desired of him.

1 JOHN 5:14-15

C learly in these two verses we have what we may accurately describe as a kind of postscript to the letter. The Apostle has already told us in the thirteenth verse the reasons that prompted him to write his letter at all, and he really had finished it at the end of that verse. But like many another letter writer, he felt it was essential to write a postscript. That, of course, happened because John was so concerned about the condition and the happiness and the welfare of the people to whom he was writing.

That is the great difference between the Scriptures and a work of art. Artistically, I suppose, a postscript is not a good thing, but the men who wrote these epistles were not interested in the art of writing as such. It was not the form that mattered—it was the content and the truth, Knowing the hard life of these people, John is anxious for them, and so he adds a postscript. In his great wisdom he wants to draw certain deductions from what he has already been saying. So what we have in these verses from the fourteenth to the end is just a series of these deductions. It is a sign, again, of a very good teacher that he summarises all he has been saying. These, he says, are the things that we can therefore proceed to act upon as a result of all that we have been laying down.

His first deduction is this whole subject of confidence in prayer. 'This is the confidence that we have in him'—in the light of all we have been saying—'that, if we ask any thing according to his will, he heareth us.' I am sure we need take no time in emphasising the vital importance of this whole subject of prayer. In many ways there is nothing more important for us in this life and pilgrimage than that we should be well instructed in this matter. I have the authority of our Lord Himself for saying that prayer is absolutely essential; He said that 'men ought always to pray, and not to faint' (Luke 18:1), the suggestion being that if you do not pray, you will faint. Prayer is essential to every pilgrim whose face is set upon glory and eternity, and without it we cannot live. Our Lord Himself spent much time in prayer, 'rising up a great while before day,' we read (Mark 1:35), for prayer.

Prayer is vital, and so the Apostle, not unnaturally, draws this as his first deduction or conclusion. 'One of the most wonderful things about all this,' says John in effect, 'is that it enables us to pray with confidence and gives us assurance in our petitions at the throne of grace and of mercy.' He has already mentioned this in passing in the third chapter, in verses 21 and 22: 'Beloved, if our heart condemn us not, then have we confidence toward God. And whatsoever we ask, we receive of him, because we keep his commandments, and do those things that are pleasing in his sight.' And here he tells us once more that nothing is more important than our prayer life and that therefore we should be certain in our minds and in our hearts with regard to this great biblical teaching with regard to prayer.

Yet there is nothing perhaps that seems to give people so much trouble and perplexity as this very question. There is nothing that leads to so much misunderstanding, and I believe that every minister and every pastor would agree in saying that he is probably questioned more frequently about this matter of prayer than about any other single subject. People seem to be in difficulty about it, and the difficulties are almost endless. I shall not deal with them all now; I am simply reminding you of the extraordinary confusion that does seem to obtain with regard to this most vital and central subject. There are those, on the one hand, who seem to feel that prayer is quite unnecessary; they say that in light of the doctrine of the sovereignty of God, how can prayer be possible? If God knows all things and everything is appointed and determined, what is the value of prayer?

But then, at the other extreme, there are people who in a spirit of fanaticism take certain biblical and scriptural statements right out of their context. They fix upon certain particular words and, on the strength of that, pray for and expect and even demand things that are almost ridiculous and thereby bring grievous distress to themselves and even ridicule upon the Christian gospel. There are people who take certain verses, which I shall quote later, and say that on that basis we are entitled to ask and to demand anything; so they try to put God to the test, as it were, and make extraordinary claims. The whole procedure leads to nothing but disappointment and perhaps a shaking of their own faith life.

We find, therefore, that the subject often presents itself as difficult and perplexing to many people. The people of whom I have just been speaking, for instance, are very fond of taking a verse like the fifteenth verse here: 'If we know that he hear us, whatsoever we ask, we know that we have the petitions that we desired of him'; and on the strength of that, they make ridiculous demands. So what do we do in the light of all this? Well, it seems to me that the first rule should be that we must observe carefully and closely what the Scripture really does show, and what the Scripture teaches concerning this subject.

The second is that we must be exceptionally careful in this matter of comparing Scripture with Scripture. The Bible never contradicts itself; therefore, in considering a subject like this, it is a good and a wise thing to gather together everything that Scripture has to tell us about the subject. We must never base our doctrine upon one statement only; or to put it in another way, our doctrine must never be so formulated as to be in conflict with any other statement of Scripture or to contradict any other clear and obvious scriptural teaching. Then, having done that, we come to certain conclusions. One conclusion is, and let me state it before I go any further, that there is an element of mystery about this question of prayer; it is one of those aspects of God's gracious dealings with us that is beyond our understanding. Now I feel like saying, 'Thank God for that!' I mean that in an ultimate and absolute sense you and I simply cannot reconcile God's omniscience and foreknowledge and sovereignty with this fact of prayer that we find so clearly taught in Scripture.

But there are so many other things one cannot understand. I cannot understand how a holy God would ever forgive or can ever forgive a single soul. I cannot understand it, but thank God, I believe it! I cannot understand the eternal mind and heart, but I thank God for a revelation that assures me that God can be just and a justifier of the ungodly. And there are many other instances and illustrations that I could give of exactly the same thing, and this question of prayer is one of them. In an ultimate philosophical sense there is an element of mystery about it, but, praise God, we are not left with philosophy. We have a gospel that comes to us in its simplicity and tells us what to do; so though our little minds cannot understand it philosophically, there is nothing that is so plain and clear in Scripture as that we are taught and exhorted to pray. Go through the Scriptures and notice the frequency of the exhortations to pray.

Not only that but, as I have already reminded you, one sees the very Son of God Himself at prayer. So if you are interested in that philosophical aspect of prayer, go immediately to the case of our Lord Jesus Christ. There is the only begotten, the eternal Son of God; there is the one who says of Himself that though He is upon earth, He is still in heaven; there is the one who says, 'I and my Father are one' (John 10:30). Why had He any need to pray; why, before choosing His disciples, did He spend all night in prayer? If you are interested in philosophical problems answer that; why was it ever necessary for the Son of God to pray so much while He was here on earth? And yet He did.

In other words, the Scripture teaches that prayer is essential and vital to us, and everywhere we are exhorted to it. Not only that, but if you read the lives of God's greatest saints in the long history of the Church, you will find that they were men and women of prayer. I believe I am right in saying that John Wesley used to say that any Christian worthy of the name should spend at least four hours every day in prayer, and he tended to judge his people by that. There has never been a man or woman of God who has been singularly used of God in this world, but that they spent much time in prayer. The nearer people are to God, the more they pray to Him; so that the testimony of the Christian Church supports the teaching of Scripture itself.

Furthermore, we have numerous incidents in Scripture of what God has clearly done by way of answer to prayer, and it seems to me that the explanation ultimately is not really difficult. The God who determines the end determines the means; and if God in His infinite wisdom is determined that He is going to bring certain things to pass as a result of and in answer to the prayers of His people, I ask with reverence, why shouldn't He? And it is there that I see the infinite condescension and kindness of God. It is His way of bringing us into and giving us a share in the work and in the glory. If you read Paul's epistle to the Philippians, you will find this. He explicitly tells them that God is doing this 'through your prayer' (Phil 1:19), so that they may come in for a share of the glory and rejoicing; and thus it was that the great Apostle who knew the mind

and will of God and was so happy in the hands of God nevertheless pleaded with the Philippians to pray for him and for his release
from prison.

This is God's way of doing things. As He has decided to order
and maintain the creation through various laws that He has put into
nature, so he has decided to work in the spiritual realm through
prayer. God could maintain the universe without the laws of nature,
but He does not choose to do it in that way. This is cause and effect;
instead of doing things directly, He does them indirectly. And it
seems to me that prayer is involved in some such way as that.
However, we must not be concerned or bothered about the philosophical aspect; it is for us to observe the plain injunctions and
exhortations of the Scriptures. It is for us to observe the lives of the
saints and to see that prayer was the very breath of their life; and if
we would follow the way the Master went, we likewise must spend
much time in prayer.

I am concerned, therefore, only to look at a certain number of
principles concerning this matter that seem to me to be obvious in
the light of the teaching of these two verses. The first is that if we
want to have real confidence in prayer, then we must know that we
ourselves are accepted by God. If I have any doubts in my mind
as to whether I am accepted by God, then prayer will be useless. I
cannot pray about any particular thing if I am unhappy about
myself or if I am doubtful as to whether God is there and whether
He is listening to me and is prepared to accept my person. I must
start with that. 'Now,' said John, 'this is one of the most glorious
things of all. These things have I written unto you . . . that ye may
know that ye have eternal life; and if you know that you have that,
then this is the confidence that we have in him, that if we ask any
thing according to his will, he heareth us.' You see the argument.
If I know that I have eternal life, then I know I am a child of God;
and if I know I am a child of God, then I know that God is my
Father. God is not some abstract X away in the heavens; God is
not just some great force spelt with a capital F; He is not some great

potentate away in the eternity of holiness. If I know I have eternal life and am a child of God, God is my Father, and I then know that He hears me.

This is a most interesting statement—'he heareth us.' Now obviously, hearing is not something mechanical, because in that sense God hears everybody. No; this word '*heareth*' is a very special one and is full of great meaning. It means that His ears are open to us; it means that His heart is enlarged towards us. There used to be a saying that so-and-so was 'the King's favourite' and that the favourite always 'had the King's ear.' That does not mean that the King could not physically hear other people who spoke to him; it meant that the man who was a favourite of the King would be especially heard by him. And that is what John means; if we have eternal life, if we are His children, we, I say it with reverence, have the ear of God—we can be confident that He is always waiting to listen to us. This was put very clearly by the blind man who was healed by our Lord. After he had been healed, the Jews questioned him as to who had done this, almost trying to prove to him that it could not have happened like that, because, they said, 'This man is a sinner.' So he replied, 'Now we know that God heareth not sinners; but if any man be a worshipper of God, and doeth his will, him he heareth' (John 9:31). 'I know,' said the blind man, 'that God has heard this man; otherwise I would not have been healed. So he cannot be a sinner because God does not hear sinners.'

What he meant was that God is not ready to do what sinners ask of Him, that God's ear is not open to them, that His heart is not enlarged towards them. But if you have accepted the whole of the teaching of this epistle and have applied the various tests propounded by John to yourself, and if as the result of all that, you know you have eternal life, then you know God is always ready to listen to you. He is always ready to receive you in audience; you need never have any doubt about that. He is your Father, and He loves you with an everlasting love. The very hairs of your head are all numbered; He is concerned about you. Think of an earthly father's love and multiply that by infinity, taking all sin out of it, and that is God's attitude towards you.

Christian people, we should always approach the throne of God with confidence and, of course, always with reverence and godly fear, because He who is in heaven is our Father. Yes, but always with assurance, always with what the author of the Epistle to the Hebrews calls a holy 'boldness' (Heb 10:19). So if you like, we can translate verse 14 like this: 'This is the boldness we have with respect to Him.' Let us, therefore, never be uncertain; get that settled before you offer a single petition. Start by thanking Him that you are His child, that He has adopted you, and that you are in Christ, and therefore He delights to see you come and to hear you offering up your prayers and your petitions. We are a favourite of the King if we have eternal life.

The second principle I deduce is this: we must not only know that we ourselves are accepted—we must also know that our prayers are accepted. 'This is the confidence that we have in him, that, if we ask any thing according to his will, he heareth us. And if we know that he hear us, whatsoever we ask, we know that we have the petitions that we desired of him.' This is a really important principle. It is at this point, of course, that the danger of excess and fanaticism comes in, and it always does so because people will not observe the conditions that are laid down so plainly in the Scriptures. Let me, then, remind you of some of the conditions, and as I am trying first to make a brief comprehensive statement, I shall merely give you some headings at this point.

What, then, are the conditions that must be observed before we can be confident and assured that our prayers are accepted by God? The first is that our motive in praying must be a correct and a true one. 'Ye ask, and receive not, because ye ask amiss, that ye may consume it upon your lusts' (Jas 4:3). 'You are complaining to me,' says James, 'that your prayers are not answered, and I tell you that this is the reason.' I think we all know what is meant by that. Our prayers can be unutterably selfish; we want a blessing for ourselves or for our family—not for the glory of God, but for ourselves. It is possible for a man to ask for his ministry to be blessed so that he may consume it upon his own lusts, his own self-esteem, and he must not be surprised if his prayers are not answered. A man may ask that souls may be given as a result of his preaching, but they are not given because if they were he would be still more inflated with his own pride. Are you troubled because your prayers are not answered? Well, search your heart. Why are you praying? Why do you want your prayers to be answered? What is the reason for that particular petition; is it something purely selfish, something you can consume upon your own lusts, your own self-love? The motive must be right and clean and pure.

The second condition is faith and believing. These words were uttered by our Lord Himself: 'And all things, whatsoever ye shall ask in prayer, believing, ye shall receive' (Matt 21:22). Or listen again to James: 'If any of you lack wisdom, let him ask of God, that giveth to all men liberally, and upbraideth not; and it shall be given him. But,' says James, 'let him ask in faith, nothing wavering: for he that wavereth is like a wave of the sea driven with the wind and tossed. For let not that man think that he shall receive any thing of the Lord' (Jas 1:5-8). There is no writer in Scripture who is more maligned than James. There is nothing, quite honestly, that so frightens me as I read Scripture as the place given to faith in the writings of James. Take his statement about the prayer of faith healing the sick (5:6). Without faith, says James, your prayers will not be answered.

Again, let us examine ourselves when we are on our knees in prayer. Do we really believe, or is it a desperate cry in the dark, in the words of the poem, speaking to 'whatever gods may be'? Is it some desperate experiment, doubtful of an answer? If it is, we must not be surprised if our prayers are not answered. There must be no doubt; we must be clear about God and our relationship to Him. Our prayers must be believing and in faith.

Another condition laid down in Scripture is that we must abide in Christ and be obedient to God. Here are the words of our Lord: 'If ye abide in me, and my words abide in you, ye shall ask what ye will, and it shall be done unto you' (John 15:7). 'If ye abide in me'– the condition is there. Or you remember what John said earlier in chapter 3 of his first epistle, verse 22: 'And whatsoever we ask, we receive of him, because we keep his commandments, and do those things that are pleasing in his sight.' We must be obedient to God and His holy laws; we have no right to expect our prayers to be received and answered if we are living in known sin, or if we are doing anything that we know to be contrary to the will of God. We must keep His commandments; we must abide in Him, and His words must abide in us. Or take the condition that is given us in this verse that we are now considering: 'This is the confidence that we have in him, that, if we ask any thing according to his will, he heareth us'–it must be according to the will of God.

The last condition is that our prayers must be in the name of Christ. He Himself said, 'Whatsoever ye shall ask in my name, that will I do' (John 14:13); and, '. . . that whatsoever ye shall ask of the Father in my name, he may give it you' (John 15:16). And again, 'No man cometh unto the Father, but by me' (John 14:6). There is no value in prayer unless it is given in the name of the Lord Jesus Christ. This is an absolute, essential condition. We have no right to expect prayer to be answered otherwise; we have no reason to believe it is acceptable in the sight of God. Of course, psychologists will tell you that prayer does you good; but when you regard prayer as nothing but a psychological exercise, you are persuading yourself, and I am not talking about that. I am talking about having an audience with God the Father and having a sure knowledge that He hears and receives us.

But let me go on to the third principle. To pray with assurance, we must not only know that we are accepted and that our prayers are accepted, we must believe–indeed, we must have confidence– that our petitions are granted if we observe the conditions we have just laid down. Now this is a very striking thing. 'If we know that he hear us, whatsoever we ask, we know that we have the petitions that we desired of him.' He does not say, 'We *shall* have'; he says, we '*have* them'; we have already got them, we already possess them. This is a very remarkable and astounding statement. The people who pray truly in this world can be certain that they already have the petitions they have desired of God.

Here again, I feel, is a statement that has often been misinterpreted. People say, 'When you offer a petition to God, if you can really persuade yourself that you have already got it, you have got it.' But that, I say again, is nothing but sheer psychology; not only is it psychology, it is something even worse. It ultimately means that what determines God's answer to my prayer is my persuading myself that I have already got it. That is not the teaching of the Scripture! The teaching of Scripture is, rather, something like this: take that famous statement in Mark's Gospel, chapter 11 and verse 24 (this is the favourite text of those who misinterpret this teaching of prayer): 'What things soever ye desire, when ye pray believe that ye receive them, and ye shall have them.' 'Now,' they say, 'the only thing to do is this: persuade yourself that you receive them and you shall have them.' And they are there on their knees agonising and trying to persuade themselves that they have got it, and then in the end they find it has not happened; they persuade themselves and yet it does not take place. They ask, 'What has happened? God has broken His word,' and their whole faith is shaken.

What, then, is wrong with that interpretation? Well, I think we should interpret Mark 11:24 by considering Romans 8:26 and 27 where we read this: 'Likewise the Spirit also helpeth our infirmities: for we know not what we should pray for as we ought: but the Spirit itself maketh intercession for us with groanings which cannot be uttered.' Then notice: 'And he that searcheth the hearts knoweth what is the mind of the Spirit, because he maketh intercession for the saints according to the will of God.' So if you take those two statements together, I think that it comes to this: Mark 11:24 seems to me, in the light of Romans 8:26, to mean that when I feel a desire and a prompting and an urge to pray, if I know and believe that I have received that from God through the Holy Spirit, I can be confident that I shall have my desires and my requests.

Is that not exactly what Paul is teaching in Romans 8? So often 'we know not what we should pray for as we ought,' says Paul. So what happens? 'The Spirit itself maketh intercession for us with groanings which cannot be uttered,' and here are we just groaning and sighing in the presence of God. What is a sigh? It is something created in you by the Spirit, and the Spirit knows the mind of God, and He always prompts and urges according to the will of God. And the promise is that 'if we ask any thing' according to the will of God He hears us; and we know that if He hears, 'we have the petitions that we desired of him.' It works like this, you see: when you believe that your prayer comes to your heart from the Spirit of God, you may be sure that an answer to your prayer will also be given from God. If I am surrendered to God, and if my one concern is to please Him, as I pray I feel and know that this petition has come to me from God, and I pray with confidence, I pray with assurance.

Is that not your experience? Do you not know something of what I am trying to say? There are times when I am led to pray; I am prompted or urged to pray, and as I pray I know I have my petition, I have already received my answer. The actual answer, in practice, may not come for weeks, for years even, and yet I know I have received it. That, it seems to me, is the plain, clear teaching not only of these words but also of those parallel passages. This is often illustrated in the lives of God's saints. They may have prayed, for instance, for physical healing, and they have prayed with confidence; they have felt led and prompted to do so, and healing has taken place. Then there has been another occasion in their experience where somebody dear to them has been taken ill. They do not feel the same urge to pray, but they do pray, and the loved one is not healed. That is the sort of thing I mean; the Holy Spirit lays these things upon the hearts of men and women and works within, 'with groanings which cannot be uttered.' We do not know how to pray—there is this sort of sigh; but if you know that the Spirit is within you, you can be certain you have your answer. The Spirit will never lead you to pray about anything but that God has, in a sense, granted you that thing.

Now this just means in practise—and oh, how comforting this is—that these are the kind of things we can pray for with absolute confidence. We can pray that all the precepts, all the promises, and all the prophecies with respect to ourselves may be fulfilled in us. 'This is the will of God, even your sanctification' (1 Thess 4:3); and if you pray for sanctification, you can be sure that God will sanctify you. It is God's will that we may know His love; ask Him therefore to reveal His love to you by the Holy Spirit, and you can be certain He will do so. And the same with all these various other promises that are in the Scriptures: 'Ask, and it shall be given you; seek, and ye shall find; knock, and it shall be opened unto you' (Matt 7:7).

Are you concerned that you do not love as much as you ought? Tell Him about it, ask Him to shed His love abroad in your heart, and He will do so. Are you concerned about some sin that casts you down? Pray this confident prayer; it is the will of God that you should be delivered from sin, so pray for it. Are you concerned that your heart shall be clean? Well, offer David's prayer ('Create within me a clean heart, O God; and renew a right spirit within me,' Psa 51:10), and I assure you, on the Word of God and on His character, that He will answer you, and the blood of Christ will cleanse you from all sin and all unrighteousness. Go through your Bible and make a list of the promises of God to you; then take them to God, use them in His presence, plead them, and you can be quite certain that you have your petition. You already possess it, and in His own time and way God will give you a full realisation of it and a full enjoyment of it.

That, then, is the first deduction that we draw from this blessed knowledge that we have eternal life and that we are children of

God. It transforms prayer; prayer no longer becomes an uncertain experiment, something done in desperation. No! We get down on our knees, and we know we speak to our Father, the Father of our Lord Jesus Christ, the one who loved us so much as to send His Son to the death of the cross for us. We come to Him knowing that; and then, knowing that our prayers are according to His will, we pray with confidence. We believe we have the answer, and we rise up calm and quiet and rejoicing and go on our way, leaving it to Him to grant us the precise performance of the petition in practice, but being certain that He has not only heard us, but that He has even answered us.

May God grant us this assurance, this holy boldness in prayer so that whatever our condition, we may take it to the Lord in prayer and do so confidently.

12

Prayer for the Brethren

If any man see his brother sin a sin which is not unto death, he shall ask, and he shall give him life for them that sin not unto death. There is a sin unto death: I do not say that he shall pray for it. All unrighteousness is sin; and there is a sin not unto death.

1 JOHN 5:16-17

We have here the second of the deductions that the Apostle draws from this great doctrine of the assurance of salvation and the possession of eternal life. He has told us, you remember, in the thirteenth verse that this is the great concern that he had in mind when he came to write the letter–the controlling thought. The most important thing in this life and world, according to John, is that we should know that we have eternal life; that has been the great theme that he has demonstrated in various ways. But here the Apostle puts it especially in terms of this confidence and assurance in prayer; and as we saw in our consideration of verses 14 and 15, he there drew the first deduction about our own personal, private prayer, when we ourselves are faced with difficulties and problems in a world like this–a world that, he is going to remind us again in the nineteenth verse, lies in wickedness or in the wicked one. When we are beset by trials and temptations, what can be more important than that we should know the way into the presence of the Father and should go there with confidence?

That is John's first deduction, and we have worked that out. But now he goes on to a second, and this has a reference to our prayers for one another, our prayers for the brethren. 'If any man see his brother sin a sin which is not unto death, he shall ask . . .' Now one cannot really look at this statement without again being impressed by the writer's method; we have already seen it so many times, and here is another example of it. John, in his whole thinking and outlook, was clearly controlled by certain basic principles and considerations, and he moves naturally and inevitably from the one to the other. You see, he cannot talk about our personal prayer without immediately thinking of prayer for the brother or sister also; how often have we seen him doing exactly this same thing.

In other words, the tests of life are not only that I should be in the right relationship to God, but that I should also be in the right relationship to my brother—brotherly love once more. After my love to God and my relationship to Him comes my relationship to the brethren. Of course, this is a great, central biblical doctrine: 'Thou shalt love the Lord thy God with all thy heart, and with all thy soul, and with all thy strength, and with all thy mind; and thy neighbor as thyself' (Luke 10:27). It is all there, but here, in particular, the reference is to the Christian brethren, those who are members of the same household of faith and of the same family of believers. And here that is what John is concerned to emphasise; he is controlled by these things.

Let me put it to you like this in a picture: we are among a number of Christian people in a world like this. We know that we are of God and that the whole world lies in the evil one, and we are a company of people marching through this wilderness. Now, we are in fellowship with God; we are walking with Him; we have fellowship with the Father and His Son, Jesus Christ, and with one another. And as we go on, nothing is more important than that these relationships should be maintained in the right way. We are concerned, obviously, about our own condition; we must be sure that we are right with God. But our concern does not stop at that— we must be concerned about the whole family. We must have this view of ourselves as Christian people, God's people–as members of the Church, in which we see ourselves as God's household, God's family. We must have a great and jealous concern about that family; our desire should be that everybody in it should be enjoying the full benefits of this great salvation and are marching together to Zion with God. So we should be very concerned that we ourselves do not fall, and we should be equally concerned that our brother or sister should not fall.

That is the New Testament concept; it is this wonderful picture of a family of people and every one of them concerned about the other. Now in this particular connection, John is concerned to emphasise the importance of prayer for a brother who may fall or fail. And once more his great doctrine is the assurance with which we should offer such a prayer, having already emphasised that we should be certain that our petitions are granted to us personally if they are in accordance with the will of God. But now he makes a tremendous claim and says that if we truly pray for this brother who has fallen into 'the sin not unto death,' we shall give him life as it were–a wonderful statement showing the effectiveness of prayer that is truly prayed on behalf of the brethren.

But I need scarcely remind you that the Apostle puts this statement, this doctrine, in such words and in such language that its main effect has often been to cause perplexity and considerable misunderstanding and trouble in the minds of many individuals in the Church. These words have often engaged the attention of men and women. What exactly do they mean, 'a sin unto death' and 'a sin not unto death'?

Now here again it seems to me that I must make one glancing comment as I pass on. Have you noticed how it happens that some of these most thorny problems in connection with the life of faith, the Christian life, are to be found in the writings of John? Take, for instance, the particular ones we have discovered in working through this epistle. How often has that first chapter been a bone of contention over the words, 'If we say that we have no sin, we deceive ourselves' and so on. Then take some of those statements in the third chapter where he says, 'Whosoever is born of God doth not commit sin'; all the argument about perfectionism really comes from that. And then we have had those various statements that we have been considering recently in this fifth chapter about the three witnesses. And it is interesting to observe that some of these difficult problems seem to have arisen from various statements made in the writings of John rather than in the writings of the Apostle Paul.

I mention this in passing merely so that those who are interested in these matters, as I think we all should be, and those who are especially interested in the question of inspiration, might pause and just ponder it. What is the precise relationship of that fact to the doctrine of inspiration? Why should these statements almost invariably be things said by John rather than by one of the other writers? It does not invalidate for a moment the doctrine of inspiration, but it does show very clearly that the doctrine of verbal inspiration does not mean a mere mechanical dictation. The personality of the writer is left as it was, and the individual characteristics of style and mode of thought remain, whereas the truth is guaranteed and controlled. There are these interesting variations. I have often queried whether it is right at all to compare and contrast the writings of these different writers, but people have done so. They say that John is more profound than Paul, and I mention this word in passing to people who hold that view: this way of putting things *is* more profound than the other way, and the logic of the great Apostle to the Gentiles is not something superior, if we can make such comparisons, to this more poetical, mystical style of the Apostle John. However, that point is not vital to salvation, nor is it vital as a doctrine, though it is a matter of interest.

So then, seeing that we have here once more one of those typical statements by this particular writer, let us be careful how we approach it. And again the whole secret is that we should observe carefully what he does and what he does not say. Instead of rushing off into particular theories and views, let us clearly observe the statement of the Apostle. So let me put it in the form of a question: what are the conditions of effectual prayer for the brethren? That is the theme, and we must never lose sight of it. And here, as I see it, are the answers. The first is that we must be in right relationship with the brethren; and the first thing here, obviously, is that we must realise that he is a brother. You see, here is the picture: there is the infant church to which John is writing. He is an old man, and he is about to leave them, and he is concerned about their welfare and happiness. 'Now,' he says, 'in a sense you must look after one another's interest. Remember, you are brethren; so if you see anyone who is a member of the church fall into sin, pray. He is a brother, not an outsider. If you believe you have eternal life, if all these others have the same life, you must be brothers.'

That is the deduction; it is a perfect theological deduction. Once more, Christian people are not merely a collection of individuals who may hold certain views in common and come together for certain purposes. Not at all! According to the New Testament we are to realise we are brothers and sisters; we belong to the same Father; we are partakers of the same divine nature; we have this intimate relationship of blood, as it were, than which nothing can be deeper or stronger. So we must look at one another as brothers and sisters; this is a family relationship. And that, of course, leads in turn to this: we must be concerned about one another; we should be exercising a watchful care and interest in one another; we should have a real concern about one another.

Of course, John does not mean by that that we should be busybodies; that is condemned in the New Testament. But it does mean that as members of a family we are not unnatural. As we are naturally interested in one another and love one another and are concerned about one another's welfare, so it should be with the members of the Christian Church. It should be a matter of great concern to all of us if any one of us is falling into sin, not only because it brings the Christian gospel into disrepute, but because our very love for that brother should make us concerned about him. We should be sorry; we should be grieved that he is missing so much and that he is bringing unhappiness upon himself and is putting himself into the wrong relationship to God and that he is likely to experience chastisement and punishment. We should be deeply and gravely concerned about him. We should not be impatient; we should not say, 'Why does this fellow let us down? Let him reap the consequences of his own actions.' Let us not say, 'We will carry on whatever he may do.' No; 'bear ye one another's burdens,' said the Apostle Paul (Gal 6:2), meaning exactly the same thing. Or again, 'Look not every man on his own things, but every man also on the things of others. Let this mind be in you, which was also in Christ Jesus' (Phil 2:4-5); Christ did not consider Himself but considered you. That other man is a brother, and we must be greatly concerned for him and his welfare.

And then the next thing John tells us in this reference to the brother is that we shall 'ask' for him before God. Now this word '*ask*' is a very strong one. 'If any man see his brother sin a sin which is not unto death, he shall ask, and he shall give him life for them that sin not unto death.' The word really means 'beseech'; it means that we should be urgent in prayer, that we should always be in an agony of prayer; it should be a fervent prayer. Now we all know what that kind of prayer is for ourselves. When we are in some desperate plight or condition we do not merely ask, we beseech—we agonize before Him. 'Do that for your brother,' says John; 'implore; be urgent and fervent. Do not cease, as it were, until the brother is restored.' That is the way to pray for the brethren.

So there, I say, we have this wonderful picture of the life of the Church; that is John's conception of a Church.

Brother clasps the hand of brother,
Stepping fearless through the night.

Bernhardt Ingemann

Christians are meant to be realising their unity, their oneness, their relationship–knowing something of the glory to which they are marching–bound together by this great love not only for the Father and the Son and the Holy Spirit, but for one another also. Because of their privileged and unique position, they exercise this watchful care; and if a brother falls, they 'restore such a one in the spirit of meekness,' remembering that they also have their weaknesses. They bear one another's burdens remembering while they do so that 'Every man shall bear his own burden' (Gal 6:1-5); they bear one another's sin. The New Testament is full of that–this oneness, living in this great concern and this great fellowship of prayer for one another. That is the relationship that must be personal before our prayers for one another can be efficacious.

But now let us turn to the second principle, which is the difficult one. The second great principle controlling this matter is that we must have a clear view of the nature of sin. We must be perfectly clear about this because John immediately introduces qualifications: 'If any man see his brother sin a sin which is not unto death'–he must know what is meant by that–'he shall ask, and he shall give him life for them that sin not unto death.' Then, 'there is a sin unto death: I do not say he shall pray for it. All unrighteousness is sin: and there is a sin not unto death.' Let us, then, approach these statements one by one. Here, it seems to me, is what we can say with confidence about the nature of sin. First, 'all unrighteousness is sin'; anything that is not righteous is sin. Anything that is not living according to God's way of life for us is sin; anything that is a departure from God's will and purpose and desire for us is sin.

Now, John undoubtedly makes that statement because, once more, he is anxious to counter the false doctrines of perfectionism

134   LIFE IN GOD

and antinomianism that he has dealt with so frequently. He was
concerned about those people who say, 'Because I am a Christian,
because I have the love of God in my heart, I no longer sin; I am
free from it.' 'All unrighteousness is sin,' says John; 'do not listen to
people who talk like that. If you see your brother doing something
that is patently wrong, that is sin, and he needs your prayer.'
Likewise with the people who are guilty of antinomianism, who say
that such things do not matter to the Christian, and who say that
because they are Christians, their actions, as it were, are irrelevant—
that it is the flesh that sinned, not themselves. 'Oh no!' says John;
'all unrighteousness is sin; anything which we ourselves recognise
as unworthy or imperfect is sin and nothing else. You must not call
it weakness or indiscretion—it is sin; it is a violation of God's law,
and anything that is a violation of God's law is sin.' He has told us,
you remember, in the third and fourth chapters[1] that the seed of
unrighteousness is sin. There is no need to argue about this, he
says; all that is the simple truth concerning us; we know that sin is
the transgression of the law—those are his various statements. That
is the first thing.

     The second statement about sin is this: all sin interrupts the life
of fellowship with God. I test that in this way: 'If any man see his
brother sin a sin which is not unto death, he shall ask, and he shall
give him life for them that sin not unto death.' So it is obvious that
this brother, who has sinned 'a sin which is not unto death' has
somehow or another interrupted his life of fellowship with God.
And the result of our prayer for such a man, says John, is that in
effect we are going to be able to give back to him this life that has
been interrupted—from which I draw the negative deduction that
all sin interrupts our life of fellowship with God. The normal
Christian life is a life of uninterrupted fellowship and communion
with Him. 'This is life eternal, that they might know thee the only
true God, and Jesus Christ, whom thou has sent' (John 17:3). The
moment we sin, there is a cloud, as it were, over that knowledge;
there is a losing of God's face for the time being, and the fellowship

has been interrupted. You find that in the first chapter of this epistle: 'God is light, and in him is no darkness at all. If we say that we
have fellowship with him, and walk in darkness, we lie, and do not
the truth' (1:5-6). That is always the effect of sin; it interrupts this
blessed communion and fellowship, and for the time being we seem
to be lifeless and cold.

I need not press this; we all must know it in experience, and it
is perhaps one of the most delicate and sensitive tests of whether
we are Christians or not. When we fall into sin, what grieves us
most of all is not the sin we have done, but the fact that we have
hurt the Person. An interruption has come into the fellowship, and
we, as it were, feel we are dead and have lost the face of God. What
a terrible statement about sin; what an exhortation to us to watch
and pray; what an urge to us to be wary and to walk circumspectly
in this world! That is what sin does; it comes between you and the
one who loves you with an everlasting, eternal love. It is the thing
that will rob you of the smile and the face of God; oh, what a horrible, foul, ugly thing it is.

That is always the effect of sin, but that brings us to the crucial
statement: 'there is a sin unto death.' What is this? Now, it is here
that the discussion has arisen. I do not think that we need to spend
much time with it because the main points can be reduced to a very
small compass. There are those who suggest that the whole thing
is quite simple and that John is merely referring to what the Apostle
Paul speaks of in the passage on the communion of the Lord's
Supper. He exhorts the people, when they come to the Table of the
Lord, to examine themselves, and he gives various reasons for this.
One is that it is because some people do not examine themselves
that 'many are weak and sickly among you, and many sleep' (1 Cor
11:30); and 'sleep' there means death. There are those, says the
Apostle Paul, who in a sense are dead because of this lack of self-
examination. So these people say that is what John is referring to
here. He is referring to the people who have sinned in such a way
that it leads to their physical death.

Now that seems to me to be an utterly impossible and a totally inadequate explanation, because when John talks of giving life to the brother who has not sinned unto death, he is not thinking of physical life. He is obviously thinking of spiritual life, and the whole context and connotation, therefore, must be determined by that. He is referring to spiritual death and not physical death, and I can prove that still further. I am told that I must pray for the man who has sinned not unto death; but John tells me, 'I do not pray for the man who has sinned a sin unto death.' Well, if sinning unto death means physical death, how do I know the man is going to die? What is the point of telling me to pray for a man who is not going to die? Clearly, therefore, it is a useless commandment. No; this has reference beyond any doubt to a spiritual condition, a spiritual condition that you and I are capable of praying about.

'There is a sin unto death,' says John, and surely it must be that to which he has referred so frequently in his letter. It is the doctrine of the antichrists, the thing he has been emphasising so much. 'Beloved,' he says, 'believe not every spirit, but try the spirits whether they are of God: because many false prophets are gone out into the world. Hereby know ye the Spirit of God: Every spirit that confesseth that Jesus Christ is come in the flesh is of God: And every spirit that confesseth not that Jesus Christ is come in the flesh is not of God: and this is that spirit of antichrist, whereof ye have heard that it should come; and even now already is it in the world' (4:1-3). And, you remember, he has also already dealt with this at great length in the second chapter: 'Little children, it is the last time: and as ye have heard that antichrist shall come, even now are there many antichrists; whereby we know that it is the last time.' Then he says, 'They went out from us, but they were not of us; for if they had been of us, they would no doubt have continued with us: but they went out, that they might be made manifest that they were not all of us' (2:18-19).

That is it; that is what he is talking about. There were people in the early church who claimed to be Christian members of the church, but they had gone out. They had left the church; they had denied this doctrine concerning Jesus as the Son of God and Jesus as the Christ. And that is why, in a sense, John writes his letter to safeguard against that. It is a terrible thing that a man should deny that Jesus is the Son of God. In other words, it seems perfectly clear to me that John here is simply repeating that teaching of the Lord concerning blasphemy against the Holy Ghost of which we read at the beginning of Matthew 12 and in the sixth chapter of the Epistle to the Hebrews. It is a wilful rejection of the teaching of the Holy Spirit as to the true nature and Messiahship of Jesus, the denying of Christ as to His true nature. That is what is meant by the sin against the Holy Ghost, and that is what John means by 'a sin unto death.'

Now let me elaborate that a little more closely, because it has so often caused people grievous trouble. Clearly this is something that cannot exist in unbelievers generally. Unbelievers are not wilful, they are not deliberate–they are just blind and ignorant. There are many in the world today who say, 'I do not believe this gospel about Jesus being the Son of God'; they are incapable of the sin against the Holy Ghost. The people who sin against the Holy Ghost are people like the Pharisees–people who claim a knowledge and an interest and an understanding; people like those described in Hebrews 6, who had been in the church and had experienced, in general, certain of the operations of the Holy Spirit and then had turned against the gospel–they denied and denounced it and said, 'Jesus is not a man–perhaps He's even an imposter.'

That is it. These are those who come into that category of having 'tasted the good word of God, and the powers of the world to come' (Heb 6:5) and then deny them–those who claim to know and yet wilfully and deliberately denounce and reject it all; those who refuse this testimony of the Holy Spirit with regard to the Son of God. We have already seen this in this chapter; John puts it like this: 'He that believeth on the Son of God hath the witness in himself; he that believeth not God hath made him a liar; because he believeth not the record that God gave of his Son' (v 10). And God gave record of the Son, he said, through the 'water,' through the 'blood,' and through 'the Holy Ghost'; to deny this witness and evidence of the Holy Spirit with regard to Jesus of Nazareth is to make God a liar, and obviously this is an unforgivable sin.

But let me be still more particular and practical. Who are the people who are *not* guilty of the sin against the Holy Ghost? I deliberately put this negatively. Let me answer like this: those who believe they are guilty of the sin against the Holy Ghost are obviously not guilty of it. If you are afraid, my friend, that you have committed the sin against the Holy Ghost, on the basis of this exposition I say to you that you can be absolutely certain you are not guilty. To be afraid that you are guilty of it is proof that you are not. The people who are guilty are people like the Pharisees, who ridicule Jesus with contempt, who are self-satisfied and dismiss Him and say, 'This is the devil, and He is doing what He does by means of Beelzebub' (compare Mark 3:22). They were arrogant, self-satisfied, self-assured; so if you are very unhappy about this thing, you are opposite to the people who are guilty of the sin against the Holy Ghost.

But take the second thing: to be assailed by doubts and evil thoughts about the Lord Jesus Christ is not to be guilty of the sin against the Holy Ghost, and for this reason: that comes from the devil. It is a temptation; it was the sort of temptation with which the devil tempted our Lord. He said, 'If thou be the Son of God . . .' (Matt 4:3). Now this is the way you can settle that: do these evil thoughts trouble you; do you regret them; do you say, 'What can I do to get rid of them?' If you do, then you are as far away from the sin against the Holy Ghost as anyone can ever be. The people who sin against the Holy Ghost are not worried or troubled; they are absolutely certain they are right, and they pour contempt on the truth. To be worried about doubts and evil thoughts, to hate them means, I say, that you are not guilty of the sin against the Holy

Ghost; you have not sinned the sin unto death—you are the very opposite of it.

Also, the people who feel terribly unworthy and who are concerned about the fact that they are not more worthy as Christians, they, again, are not those who have committed the sin against the Holy Ghost. And lastly I would say that those who are trying to find God and wish to be found of Him, those who pray and go the place of prayer, those who delight to hear the gospel—all these are not guilty of this sin. I put it like that because I once received a letter from an anonymous writer that went as follows: 'How does one know if he or she has sinned against the Holy Ghost? Would one try to find God or to be found of God, or pray, or come to the place of prayer? Would a person who has sinned against the Holy Ghost,' asked this writer, 'do such things?' And the answer is, 'No!' Would a person who has committed this dreadful sin like to attend evangelistic meetings or bring other people to them? Would such a person ever be touched by a soul-searching sermon and have to fight the tears that will sometimes come and, when tempted to commit suicide, fear to do so because of the hereafter? And the answer in every single case is again a confident and assured, 'No!'

The people who have sinned against the Holy Ghost have gone out, said John, and they do so positively and with assurance. These are the people who have sinned the sin unto death; but troubled, tormented, humble souls who are unhappy about this thing and hate these ugly, foul thoughts, who are harassed by them and long to get rid of them, who are troubled about the imperfection of their lives and love—such people are as far away from the sin against the Holy Ghost or the sin that is unto death as it is possible for a person to be. The people who are guilty of this sin are arrogant and self-satisfied; they dismiss the gospel and do not want to hear God. That is the character of such a person, and that brings me to my final deduction.

All sin that is short of that is sin for which we can pray and pray with confidence, not only in ourselves, but in any other person.

'There is a sin not unto death'; 'the sin unto death' is that which crucifies Christ afresh, saying that He is not the Saviour, saying that His blood shed upon the cross is not the only way. That alone is 'the sin unto death,' and anything short of that is not. And when men and women have not sinned that sin, with love and compassion, with concern and with urgency we not only *can* pray for them—we *should* pray for them. And we have this blessed assurance that if we pray thus with faith, knowing the access we have to Him, we shall be able, as it were, to restore that brother and sister; God will see that our prayer is the means of restoring them to the full life of fellowship. They will continue with us in this glorious march towards Zion, and we shall rejoice together more than ever at the wondrous grace of God that not only forgives us at the beginning, but that continues to forgive us and to heal our backsliding and to restore us to the joyous life of fellowship.

13

Safe in the Arms
of Jesus

We know that whosoever is born of God sinneth not; but
he that is begotten of God keepeth himself, and that wicked
one toucheth him not.

1 JOHN 5:18

We come here to the first of three statements that are
made by the Apostle John in this postscript to his letter,
each of which starts with this confident assertion 'we
know.' He has been dealing with prayer, our own personal private
prayer and our prayer for others; and having said all that, he comes
to this statement of the eighteenth verse. You will see, in a manner
that is very characteristic of himself, that the Apostle takes up a
thought and expounds it. I have often pointed out as we have
worked through this letter that really the way to understand John
is to remember that his method is rather that of the poet or musi-
cian than that of the logician or one who uses the more orthodox
type of reasoning. He never seems to start out by laying down a
number of propositions and then treating them one by one. He
rather takes up a theme and, in dealing with that, mentions a cer-

tain aspect, and that, as it were, suggests another major theme to him, so he takes it up.

Now here is a perfect illustration of that. John is really setting out to take up the theme of praying for one another and the thought in particular of praying for brothers and sisters when they fall into sin. But that raises a question in his mind. He has said in verse 17 that 'all unrighteousness is sin,' and that 'there is a sin not unto death,' and so you must pray for a man who is in that condition. But then he says to himself, 'I must qualify that a little; I must make sure they are still clear about this whole question of sin in the life of a Christian.' So he gives a special statement: 'We know that whosoever is born of God sinneth not; but he that is begotten of God keepeth himself, and that wicked one toucheth him not.'

Now we must stop, just for a moment, at this affirmation, 'we know.' There are certain things, according to this writer and according to the whole of the New Testament, about which there is no need for discussion; there are certain things, as it were, that are axiomatic in the Christian life. You remember the axioms in your books on geometry? There are certain things laid down, and then you build your propositions on them; but these things themselves are basic postulates and propositions. And here are some such things, according to John; and, therefore, as Christian people we must never be in doubt about them. These are the things that we as Christian people 'know,' so that in a sense we can say that if we do not know, we are not Christians. 'Whatever may happen to you,' says John, 'wherever you may find yourselves, here are things that are simple absolutes in your life—*we know*!' We know this first; we know in the next place 'that we are of God, and the whole world lieth in wickedness [or, in the wicked one]'; and we also know that 'the Son of God is come, and hath given us an understanding, that we may know him that is true; and we are in him that is true, even in his Son Jesus Christ. This is the true God, and eternal life.'

Now it is, of course, a most excellent and valuable thing to isolate great principles like these. There are many points that are

debatable and disputable in the Christian life and experience, but
there are certain things that can always be isolated and extracted
and laid down as postulates, and here are some. And surely we misunderstand the whole message of this epistle if by now we have not
come to see that these things are absolutes. So here we come then
to the first of them—the Christian and sin.

Once more I must indicate that this subject has caused a great
deal of confusion and misunderstanding. It has led to a great deal
of disputation—very largely, again, because of the way in which this
particular writer states his case. We have already seen in passing
how it is interesting to observe that some of these thorny points of
dispute in connection with the Christian life do arise from statements made by John rather than by the Apostle Paul, and this is
entirely due, as I suggested, to that extraordinary type of thought
and mind that he had. It is simply a question of the natural personality of the writer that was used by the Holy Spirit; the truth is
clear and plain, but we have to pay attention to the form in which
it is conveyed.

So there is a difficulty here. The whole doctrine of perfectionism has often been based upon this particular verse and upon its
parallel statement in the ninth verse of chapter 3, which reads like
this: 'Whosoever is born of God doth not commit sin; for his seed
remaineth in him: and he cannot sin, because he is born of God.'
That is the great text of perfectionists throughout the centuries,
with this one to support it because it is virtually a repetition of the
same thing. So it is necessary once more that we should pay close
attention to exactly what the Apostle does say. Not only that; we
must be exceptionally careful to take the context into consideration.

Nothing, incidentally, is more dangerous in reading or inter-
preting Scripture than to take a single statement right out of its context and elaborate a theory or doctrine upon it. That has generally
been what has happened in every heresy and in every error in the
long history of the Church. It is this fatal habit of men and women
of jumping on to texts, as it were, and saying, 'The Bible says this—

therefore . . . ' And they forget the context; they forget that Scripture must always be compared with Scripture; that Scripture never contradicts itself, and that there is a homogenous collation and unity about the message of the Bible from beginning to end. So it is important that we should bear that in mind as we come to this particular verse that is engaging our attention now.

So let us look at this first thing about which John tells us, 'We know; we are certain beyond dispute.' It is a comprehensive statement and obviously divides itself into three subsidiary statements. There is no difficulty about subdividing this verse—it does it for us itself. The first statement that he makes is this: 'Whosoever is born of God sinneth not.' 'We know that,' John says; 'there is no need to argue—there is no need for you to stop and consider it—we know it.' But the question is, what exactly is it that we thus 'know'? Well, it is the same thing as he tells us in chapter 3, verse 9.

Let me suggest what it does *not* mean. It cannot mean that whoever is born of God is incapable of sin. At first sight it looks as if John is indeed saying that whosoever is born of God does not sin—'sinneth not'—which has led many of the perfectionists to say they cannot sin. John uses that term in chapter 3, where he says that he does not sin because 'his seed remaineth in him.' So people have argued and said, 'As a Christian I cannot sin. John does not say I must not, but that I cannot. Therefore, I am incapable of sin as a Christian; it is impossible to me.' And they would therefore explain away in terms of the flesh various things that are pointed out to them that they have done and that are clearly a transgression of the law.

But surely the answer to all that, in this verse here, is just the context. If it is true to say that a Christian is one who is born again, who is born of God and is incapable of sin, why should John, as it were, have wasted his breath in the two previous verses by exhorting us to pray for our brother who *does* fall into sin? Such an exhortation is ridiculous if he is here saying that the Christian is incapable of sin. So it cannot mean that.

'Well,' says somebody else, 'I wonder whether it means not so much that the man who is born of God is incapable of sin, but that he does not fall into sin. It is possible, but he just does not do it. It is not that he has been made so absolutely perfect that he cannot sin, but that he is placed in a position in which it is possible for him not to sin.' Now there are two little Latin phrases: *non posse peccare* and *posse non peccare*, which mean either it is not possible for a Christian to sin or it is possible for him not to sin, and you can see the difference between the two. Is John saying that a Christian is someone who in actual practice and as a matter of fact does not sin? And once more it seems to me that the answer is precisely the same—that if the Christian does not sin, it would be unnecessary to exhort us to pray for the brethren who do fall into sin. Now the power that is offered to us in the Bible can keep us from sin—that is a different thing. But all I am concerned to indicate now is that John does not say that the Christian, the one who is born of God, does not fall into or commit particular acts of sin.

So what does he say? Well as I understand it, the only conceivable way of understanding the whole of this epistle is to repeat what I said when we considered chapter 3, verse 9.[1] What John means is that whosoever is born of God does not go on continuing in a state of sin; he does not continue practising sin. He is not interested in action at this point; he is interested in *condition*. He is concerned about the state of the Christian, not in the particular action of the Christian. And what he is asserting, therefore, is that whosoever is born of God is in a different condition with respect to sin from whosoever is not born of God. Men and women who are not born of God lie 'in the wicked one,' in the evil one. They are in the dominion of Satan. Their whole life is a life of sin; they dwell in it, it is their realm, and they inhabit it. But those who are born of God are no longer in that state; they have been taken out of it.

Look at this in terms of what John has told us in the first chapter; he is very fond of thinking in this way. He says that the man or woman who is not born of God is one who walks, or lives, in the realm of darkness; but the one who is born of God walks in the light with God. That is the first thing that John has in mind here. He says that those who are begotten of God do not continue in a state of sin; they may fall into sin—he has just been reminding us that the brethren, alas, do this—but they do not dwell there; that is not their condition. That surely is the only adequate explanation of this statement.

The way to look at this is to think of it as the two realms, the realm of darkness and the realm of light, the dominion of Satan and the kingdom of God and of His Christ. Or if you prefer it, I sometimes like to think of it in the sense of being down or being up. The men and women who are not born of God are those who live on a low level in life. They make occasional efforts to improve themselves, and they attempt to raise themselves for a while; but back they go. That is their level, down there. But Christians, those who are born of God, have been elevated; they have been raised up by Christ to a new height, so that the level of life on which they are living is up there. Now, unfortunately, they occasionally fall into sin; but that does not mean they continue to live down there. They fall, they repent, and they are received back again to the height and the level of their life.

So what John is concerned to emphasise is the level of life on which we are living. And his assurance is that those who are born of God no longer live on the sinful level, but on the higher level. Their whole realm is different and is changed; that is the position to which they belong. Alas, they may fall, they may lapse, but they do not continue on the ground, as it were. They belong to that other realm; that is their native sphere. He 'sinneth not' in the sense that he does not continue in sin, he does not keep on; or to use John's favourite word, he does not 'abide' in sin. The apostle is interested in character, not in particular action and conduct, at this point.

Perhaps I can put it again in the form of an illustration. I happened to be talking to a minister recently, and he was telling me about his two little children. He was telling me, with shame, how these little children could be a bit of a trial when he was trying to prepare his sermons. He said, 'You know, before my conversion I had a very bad temper, and it was a great trouble in my life–I could not control it. But I thought that once I was converted I would get rid of that for ever. But,' he said, 'I find myself still falling into it.' He is no long a bad-tempered man, he has been delivered out of that; but he continually has to watch it–there is a tendency to fall back into it. But he does not stop there; the thing that grieves him is that he ever loses his temper at all. Before his conversion he was doing nothing else; it was then his natural state and condition. But it is now an exception; he is living on a new level. He does not abide in this state of irritability; it is not his character any longer. 'Whosoever is born of God does not continue in sin'–does not abide in sin. That is the real meaning of the word, and that is the first thing of which we can be certain and which we 'know.'

But let me go on to the second statement, which is much more difficult. 'We know that whosoever is born of God sinneth not; but [or because] he that is begotten of God keepeth himself.' Now here again is a statement that is difficult, not, if I may so put it, in a doctrinal or theological sense, but simply as a matter of exposition; and it is entirely due, once more, to the whole question of the difference in the various texts of the New Testament. You remember that we have already had occasion to emphasise the difference between textual criticism of the New Testament and the so-called higher criticism. There are a number of manuscripts, and there are minor differences that do not affect ultimate truth, but they do affect the interpretation of a particular statement.

Here is an example of this. The Revised Version here reads, 'He that was begotten of God keepeth him.' Can you see the difference? The Authorised Version seems to suggest that 'whosoever is born of God does not sin because he keeps himself'–he looks after himself. But the other version suggests that 'whosoever is born of God does not sin because he that was begotten of God keeps him.'

Now I think there can be very little doubt but that in this instance the Revised Version is probably right, because it seems to me to be more in accord with what we have in the whole text here, with the whole object that John has in mind, and, indeed, with the teaching of the whole of the New Testament. It is not that these different versions contradict each other at all; they are both true in a sense, but it is just a question of what John is emphasising at this point. 'Whosoever is [has been] born of God sinneth not.' Why? Because 'he that *was* begotten' now 'is begotten'; John has changed his tense. Now surely this change is important, and that is why we must accept the translation of the Revised Version at this point. 'He that was begotten' stands alone and is none other than the Son of God, our Lord and Saviour, Jesus Christ.

Then again, we have another difference. 'He that was begotten of God,' says the Revised Version, 'keepeth *him*,' not 'himself.' Once more this is purely a question of these different manuscripts; but if 'was begotten' is a reference to the Lord Jesus Christ, I think we must agree that 'him' is correct here. So it comes to this: the Authorised Version suggests that the begotten of God does not sin because he keeps himself, while the Revised Version suggests that he that is born of God does not sin because the Son of God keeps him. Now this word *keepeth* is very important, and it is a great word. It means that He watches over him, takes care of him, keeps His eye on him; it means that He observes him attentively. Now I am sure that that is what the Apostle wanted to say at this point. He was writing, an old man, to these people who were tempted and tried and harassed with troubles outside and inside the Church. And this is what he wanted them to know—that the only begotten Son of God is watching over them; He is keeping them in that sense. He is the watchman of Israel; He is never asleep but always awake.

Let me show you that this must be what John is anxious to convey here. This statement is repeated in John 17; it is the same writer, and I am sure he had the same idea in his mind here. But we have it in his Gospel even before that, where our Lord Himself says about His sheep, 'Neither shall any man pluck them out of my hand' (John 10:28). He is going to keep them. But then listen to Him in His high priestly prayer: 'Holy Father,' He says, 'keep through thine own name those whom thou hast given me' (John 17:11)–keep them. Then He goes on to say, 'While I was with them in the world, I kept them in thy name: those that thou gavest me I have kept'–in effect, 'I have looked after them'–'and none of them is lost, but the son of perdition'–that is prophecy, he has gone. 'I pray not that thou shouldest take them out of the world,' He adds, 'but that thou shouldest keep them from the evil' (which means, 'from the evil one') (vv 12, 15)–the very thing John says in this verse. Surely, then, we are confronted here by that statement. It is the same thing of which Jude reminds us: 'now unto him that is able to keep you from falling, and to present you faultless before the presence of his glory with exceeding joy' (Jude 24). That is it!

This is the thing you find so constantly in our hymns–the celebration of the fact that the God who has kept and held His people in the past is still our God.

> *Guide me, O Thou great Jehovah,*
> *Pilgrim through this barren land;*
> *I am weak, but Thou art mighty,*
> *Hold me [or keep me] with Thy powerful hand.*

> William Williams

Augustus Toplady's confidence, too, is that Christ is his keeper; He looks after him:

> *A sovereign Protector I have,*
> *Unseen, yet for ever at hand,*
> *Unchangeably faithful to save,*
> *Almighty to rule and command.*

He smiles, and my comforts abound;
His grace as the dew shall descend,
And walls of salvation surround
The soul He delights to defend.

This is the other side of the prayer,

I need Thee every hour;
Stay Thou near by.

Why?

Temptations lose their power
When Thou art nigh.

Annie Sherwood Hawks

This is one of the great consoling, comforting doctrines that we find in the New Testament—praise God! When we realise our weakness and helplessness in this difficult contradictory world, what is our final consolation save this that the Apostle Paul writes in Romans 5:10: 'For if, when we were enemies, we were reconciled to God by the death of his Son; much more, being reconciled, we shall be saved by his life.' If He died to save us, He will keep us, He will look after us; 'He that was begotten of God keepeth him.' 'Let us remember that then,' says John; 'let us be so certain of it that we can use the claim that we know it.' Let us be sure that wherever we are and however hard pressed and difficult our circumstances, we know that the Son of God is the shepherd and the guardian of our souls; that He is watching over us, He is keeping His eye upon us, He will not suffer us to be tempted above that we are able to bear but always 'will with the temptation also make a way to escape' (1 Cor 10:13)—thank God for that! He who was begotten of God is keeping us; that is why we do not dwell or continue or abide in a state of sin.

But that brings us to the last statement, the third great term: 'that wicked one [or evil one] toucheth him not.' Once more we have to be careful about a word, and here it is the word '*toucheth*.' Now, what one normally means by touching is putting your hand lightly upon somebody; but that is not the meaning of this word. The commentators all point out, very rightly, that John only used this word in one other connection, and you will find it in the twentieth chapter of his Gospel and the seventeenth verse, where, after His resurrection, our Lord was recognised by Mary. Mary took hold of Him, and He said to her, according to our translation, 'Touch me not.' He said, 'Don't keep clinging to me, Mary; don't hold on to me, for I am not yet ascended to my Father.'

Now, that is what John says here. 'That wicked one' does not get hold of those who are born of God; that evil one does not cling to them, does not get them into his embrace; he does not get them back into his clutches. Again, what a wondrous promise this is! You see how it fits in with the previous doctrine? If we just think of that word 'toucheth' with its usual connotation, it would virtually be saying that a Christian cannot be tempted, but that would patently be wrong. John does not say that we know that because we are born again we will never be touched in that sense. No, the devil will tempt us, that wicked one will try us; he may torment us, he may make us wretched and miserable. He will do his best to depress us and make us unhappy. Yes; but he will never get us back into his clutches. That is what John is saying. He can do many things to us, but he will never hold us again.

'They overcame him,' says the book of Revelation, 'by the blood of the Lamb, and by the word of their testimony' (Rev 12:11). He tried to get them back, he almost persuaded them, but he could never get them back into his grip—they 'overcame.' Yes, he can tempt us, he can even entice us in our folly to fall into acts of sin; but never again will we be held by him. Redemption cannot be undone; we have been delivered—we have been emancipated and set free. We belong to Christ, and we are children of God. We belong to the heavenly family, and though in our weakness and frailty we may often listen to Satan and his insinuations and suggestions, let us never forget that great word of John: 'that wicked one' will never get us back; he will never cling to us and embrace us.

The next verse says the whole thing: 'We know that we are of God, and the whole world lieth in wickedness,' in the arms of Satan. But you and I, beloved friends in Christ, will never be back there again—it is impossible. We are safe in the arms of Jesus, beyond the furthest reach of Satan; he cannot finally rob God of His possession. 'No man shall pluck them out of my hand.'

That, then, is the first thing we are to 'know,' and may God grant that we know it—that being born of God, we do not continue in sin. May God grant that we know that the Son of God is keeping an eye on us and is watching over us and is protecting us. May God grant that we may always know, when tempted by Satan, that we do not belong to him, that we need not be frightened of him, that we can resist and defy him. May we know that we can have this assurance that we are beyond his reach and his clutches, because we belong to God our Heavenly Father, to the Lord Jesus Christ, His precious Son and our Saviour, and to the Holy Ghost, whom He has given us to form Christ in us and to prepare us for the glory that awaits us.

14

The Life of the World

And we know that we are of God, and the whole world
lieth in wickedness [the wicked one].

1 JOHN 5:19

We look together now at the second of these three confident affirmations that the Apostle gathers together here
in the postscript to his letter. And this second statement
follows, I think we must agree, logically from the first. John, in
emphasising the fact that whosoever is born of God does not sin
because he is kept by the Son of God, ended by remarking that
because of all that, he could not get into the clutches of the evil one
again. And that suggests this second statement to him, that we are
of God, but the whole world lies in the clutches of that evil one.

Looked at from any angle, this is a most important and vital
statement. It is a statement of the Christian's view of life in this
world, and surely nothing can be more important than that. The
celebrated preacher Robert Murray McCheyne said of this verse—
his advice to his congregation—'Never rest until you can say this.'
Certainly, whatever our particular view may be of the statement,
we must admit that it is very typical and characteristic of the New

153

Testament. You find it everywhere; there is a very definite view of
this world in the Gospels, in the book of Acts, and in the various
epistles.

Take, again, for instance, our Lord's high-priestly prayer in
John 17, and you will find that it is just an elaboration of this particular statement. Our Lord there divides His people from those
who are of the world. He says He does not pray for the world, but
for those whom God has given Him out of the world; and His
prayer is that His people might be kept from certain influences in
that world. And you will find that implicitly in our Lord's teaching
everywhere. And again, you will find it running right through the
epistles. Take the famous Hebrews 11 with its portraits of the great
heroes of the faith and the old dispensation; what we are told about
them all is really that these men and women were declaring plainly
that they were seeking another country. They were a people apart—
unique people who had an utterly different view of life from all others. They were men and women who regarded themselves as
pilgrims and strangers and sojourners in this world; it is the same
distinction.

And you find this sometimes as an explicit exhortation: 'Come
out from among them, and be ye separate, saith the Lord' (2 Cor
6:17); 'what communion hath light with darkness?' (2 Cor 6:14);
and so on. In those places it is as an explicit injunction or exhortation. And as we have seen repeatedly in our study of this epistle,
this is a distinction that runs right through the whole letter; it is, in
a sense, a kind of basis on which John elaborates the whole of his
argument. And that is why, when we began to study this letter
together,[1] we started with this verse, because I tried to show that
there is a sense in which if we do not understand this verse, we cannot understand the whole of the epistle; so we took it as an intro-
duction. And we are back to it now, not to repeat what we said then,
but to expound it in its particular context here in this postscript.

This is, therefore, a typical New Testament statement, but you
will find exactly the same thing if you consider the subsequent his-

tory of the Christian Church after the end of the New Testament canon. I suggest to you that every period of reformation, every great time in the movement of the Holy Spirit, has been an era when this particular world view has been prominent and has been emphasised. Monasticism, for example, degenerated into something that became evil, but the original idea behind its message was based upon this clear-cut division of God's people.

Then you get it emphasised particularly at the time of the Reformation, and it was obviously the very essence of the doctrine that was emphasised by the Puritans—hence, partly the reason why they were given that name. They were not only interested in liturgical reform—they were particularly interested in this way of life which the Christian should live. Perhaps we can summarise it all by saying that this is obviously the controlling idea of *Pilgrim's Progress*. John Bunyan has once and for ever voiced the whole teaching of this verse; *Pilgrim's Progress* is nothing but a great allegory on it. So then, we see that this is one of the great basic and controlling concepts of Christian history.

Or if you prefer to look at this from the practical standpoint, I think you will have to agree again that it is of supreme importance, because it is a verse like this that really determines our attitude towards what is happening in the world at the present time. We all must be concerned with our present situation, and the problem that must arise in our mind is why the world is as it is. Now, whether we believe this verse or not determines our view of, or reaction to, the present scene; are we surprised at it, or do we expect it? Are we baffled by it, or is it in accordance with our whole outlook on the course of life in this world?

But still more personally, it is my attitude towards this verse that determines my own conduct and behaviour. I am in a world that is speaking to me and addressing me constantly in its newspapers, its books, its whole organisation of life, and its outlook. It is always making suggestions to me; its advertisements, the people with whom I speak and with whom I mix—all these are making appeals to me. So my response and reaction to all this will be determined by the fact of whether I agree with the doctrine of this verse or not.

So from every standpoint this is one of the most basic and vital statements that we must consider and that we must face. And you see at once that it confronts us with a very striking situation. Look at all the parallels in similar New Testament statements; look at those great lives in the Church in every time of revival. They all imply a clear-cut division and distinction between the Christian and the non-Christian. According to the New Testament, it should not be difficult to tell who is a Christian, for Christians are not merely people who are slightly better than others. They are not merely people who have added something to their lives. They belong to a different realm, to a different organisation; they are utterly different: 'We are of God, and the whole world lieth in wickedness.' You cannot imagine a greater contrast. Now that is the New Testament emphasis everywhere; the Christian and the non-Christian are altogether different. It is not some subtle, slight difference or change; it is a cleavage that is as clear-cut and as absolute as anything can be.

So it is obvious that what determines our view of the statement of this verse, what decides whether we can apply this verse to ourselves or not, whether we feel, like Robert Murray McCheyne, that this is the most important thing I can ever say about myself, what determines all this is clearly our view of the world and our view of the Christian. Now there are many people who are in trouble about this whole statement. There are those who feel that it implies an air of superiority and boastfulness and pride. There are people who say, 'I cannot make a statement like that; does it not suggest that you are looking down with derision upon everybody? If you say that, are you not being like the Pharisee who said, "God, I thank Thee that I am not as other men are—like this publican?" Is this not the very essence of the Pharisaical spirit of boastfulness, pride, arrogance—indeed worse, of superiority? I do not like it,' they say.

But surely that is completely to misunderstand this statement.

There was nothing further from the mind and the heart and the spirit of this Apostle. He, above all others, liked to preach the doctrine of love. The spirit here is not one of pride and arrogance; it is, rather, one of profound gratitude. The statement is one of thanks to God, and it is said with humility. Yet it must be said. And if we are in any trouble or confusion in our minds with regard to this statement, it must be due to the fact that there is something wrong in our view of the world, or something wrong in our view of the Christian, or perhaps both. That is why we must consider these two things about which the Apostle has written so frequently in this letter; and if our view of them is not in accordance with the New Testament, then we must recognise the absolute cleavage, this utter distinction.

Now I am prepared to say that perhaps the thing above everything else that is most responsible for the present state of the Christian Church is the failure to maintain this distinction. The line between the Church and the world is becoming increasingly indistinct; they are becoming so much one for many reasons. And this accounts for the weakness of the Church, her unhappiness, and her failure to influence the life of the world. Because the attitude of the man of the world is virtually, 'What have you got that I have not?' he says, 'What is the difference between us? Why should I come amongst you?'

Or put it another way: I think you will find that at every period of revival and reformation, the Church has stood out distinct and apart. That is always the way; when the Church is unique, she has the greatest influence upon the world. The tragedy of the twentieth century especially has been that the Church in her folly has been trying to accommodate herself to the world, thinking that by so doing she could attract it. But the world expects the Christian to be different, and it is right—this is the New Testament emphasis. It is nothing but a departure from New Testament doctrine that ever tries to make the Church ingratiate herself to the world; the Church is meant to be, and is, essentially different. So this means that we must go back and consider the Christian view of the world and the Christian's view of the Christian.

First, let us look at the Christian view of the world. 'The whole world,' says John, 'lieth in wickedness [or, the wicked one].' Now as we have pointed out in our study of the second chapter,[2] by 'world' John does not mean the physical organisation of the world. What the Bible always means by 'the world' is life as it is organised without God—the outlook and the mentality of mankind that is exclusive of thoughts of God; life in the world as it is controlled without, or apart from, God. Now that, you see, is a very comprehensive definition. It includes the whole life of the world, and I would emphasise this. John says '*the whole world*,' and he means it. 'The whole world' does not only mean those who dwell in the gutters of sin; it is inclusive of all life that excludes God, at its very best and highest as well as at its very worst and lowest. It is very important that we should maintain that in our minds. So then, what is our view of life in this world defined in that way?

Now, the whole object here is to emphasise the uniqueness of the Christian view, and perhaps we can do that best by putting it negatively. Let us look at some of the other views of the world, and life in the world as it is today, in order that we may emphasise and stress and contrast this uniqueness.

There are many who take a biological view of life. If you go to these people and ask them how they explain the state of the world—why it is so troubled and unhappy, what has gone wrong with it, and what is its real need—their answer is purely biological. They say that it is just a part of this process of evolution, part of the development, the growing pains that always accompany growth. You cannot expect, they say, to advance and develop without a certain amount of conflict and reaction. There are forces that have to be overcome, and these troubles in the world are but a manifestation of that. It is all right, they maintain; there is nothing to be alarmed about; childhood and youth are often a period of strain and crisis, but they are part of the inevitable process as we advance.

But to others it is purely a question of economics. There was a great deal of talk before the Second World War of 'the psychology of the economic mind.' This is a century of economics, as last century was a century of the biological; the great thing in this century is economic force. Life in this world, they say, is entirely governed and controlled by capital and labour. Indeed, there are some who think they can explain it all in terms of food! It is a question of food and an attempt to satisfy the fundamental needs of man–economics.

But then there are others who describe the whole thing in terms of politics. 'No,' they say, 'the real trouble with man is that he is a political animal, and these associations in life always need a certain amount of organisation. We have done very well, but we obviously have not perfected it, and there are certain nations that are backward, politically immature, and they need to be developed and trained.' So they, too, exhort us to be patient, because they assure us that as man is more trained politically he will solve his problems.

But still another group says that the whole problem is one of intellect. In other words, the real trouble with the world and all the troubles of mankind, they say, are due to the fact that people do not use their brains. They are foolish enough to live too much like the animal; they are not sufficiently developed. That was the great theory preached by men like H. G. Wells; that was his creed. Such people assure us that if only we gave men and women better knowledge and education, we could solve our personal problems, our national problems, and indeed our international problems.

Then the last view is what we might call the moral view. 'No,' say these last people, 'the problem of life in this world is not biological or economic or political or intellectual; the problem of life in this world is a moral one. People are taking a far too materialistic view in these days, rather than considering man in his relationship to man, man in his conception of good and evil, man in his conception as to how life should be lived. So the moral problem is the real problem for us.' Now you will notice that I am putting this moral view in the same category as the others because I am anxious to show that, in a sense, that is as far removed from the Christian view as is the biological or any of the others.

There, then, are some of the most common ideas with respect to life in this world that are current today; but there are others. Some of them may actually claim to be religious, but we have seen that to have a religious view of the world is not the same thing as to have a Christian view.

So let us turn now to this view that is entirely different from all the others. The Christian, New Testament view of life in this world is spiritual, and it is essentially different even from the moral view. Here it is: 'The whole world lieth in wickedness.' In other words, according to this view the trouble with the world is not that it just lacks certain qualities; it is not simply that it ought to be better than it is. Rather, the life of this world is controlled entirely and absolutely by an evil power, by the one who is described here as 'the wicked one.' That is what I mean when I say it is the spiritual view of life in this world.

In other words, we are facing here the biblical doctrine of sin and the biblical doctrine of the devil. Here again is something you find running through Scripture. Our Lord speaks about 'a strong man armed,' keeping his goods and palace at peace (Luke 11:21). That is typical; in other places he talks about 'the prince of this world' (John 12:31). We find this also in Ephesians 2:2, where Paul talks about 'the prince of the power of the air'; or again we find such terms as 'the god of this world' (2 Cor 4:4), or the adversary and 'the accuser of our brethren' (Rev 12:10). So my point is that if we accept the biblical view of life in this world, to believe in Satan is an absolute necessity, for the Christian view of life is a spiritual view.

We can put it like this: there is an evil person, according to the Bible, who is controlling the life of this world. We are told about him in the Old Testament. God made man perfect, and He made the world perfect—it was called Paradise. What went wrong? Well, an evil person came in—an angel of exceptional brightness and glory who had rebelled against God and set himself up against Him and attacked the very being and power of God. He, the devil or Satan, came into God's universe and tempted man; and man listened and fell. That is the cause of the trouble, according to the Scriptures. When man listened to the suggestions and insinuations of Satan, he handed himself and his world over to the dominion of Satan. And, according to this view, ever since the fall of man into sin, the devil, who is described in the categories I have mentioned, is controlling life in this world. The whole world lies in the power of the evil one. It is lying in his bosom; he is there clasping it, and he is controlling its whole outlook and all its activities and everything that happens in it.

That is the Christian view. Is that not the explanation of our ills and troubles? It is not the economic view, nor the political view. The problem is not our intellectual lack or our lack of culture; it is not even that we are not striving to be as moral as we ought to be. It is that we are controlled and the life of the world is controlled by Satan; the god of this world has blinded men and women. It is the devil who has a stranglehold upon the whole outlook and mentality and upon the whole organisation of life in the world. In other words, the world, according to Scripture, is positively evil; it is being governed by this unseen spiritual power who holds it in its grasp.

You cannot read the New Testament without coming across this concept. 'For we wrestle not against flesh and blood, but against principalities, against powers, against the rulers of the darkness of this world, against spiritual wickedness in high places' (Eph 6:12). Read about these dominions and thrones and principalities and powers that are so constantly mentioned; look at the Book of Revelation with its great struggle. What does it mean? What is behind this evil power, these figures that are used, such as beasts and others? They are but a representation of this malign power of Satan, the devil, the god of this world.

So according to this statement and according to the whole biblical teaching, the world is as it is today because it is being controlled by the devil. You remember how, when he tempted our Lord in the wilderness, one of the temptations he put before Him was this: he took Him to a high mountain and showed Him all the kingdoms of this world, and he said in effect, 'Bow down and worship me, and I will give it all to you' (Matt 4:8-9). He was making there a claim for himself, and that claim, in this spiritual sense, is true. He has mastered life in this world; he holds man under his control; 'the whole world lieth in the wicked one.'

Now I emphasise this because I know full well that there are many who not only dispute this, but who dislike it. 'Clearly,' they say, 'that is ridiculous. It is something that we can understand in a book that was written, most of it, two thousand years ago; it is typical of primitive society and primitive mentality. We can even understand it and believe it about people a hundred and fifty years ago. But how can you still go on preaching a doctrine like that? Look at the improvements in this world. Look how much less suffering and cruelty there is. Look at the factory acts and so on. Look at the care we are giving to the aged and to the ill and to the infirm. Look at our great advance and development. Are you asking us to believe that this world is under the control of the evil one and in the grasp of the devil?'

To which surely the answer is perfectly simple. Let us look at the so-called improvements. We are well aware that the acts of Parliament that have been passed in the last hundred years or so have righted many wrongs; but I would ask you to remember that they have, all of them, without a single exception, resulted directly from Christian activity. None of these things have been automatic. Take the movements for better education; take the hospitals; take the interest in health or the care for the aged, the abolition of slavery, the passing of factory acts—every one of these things has emanated from Christian sources. It has not been a development. No; these things have come from work organised by Christian men and women, often against violent opposition from those who were not Christians. We must always remember when we look at the life of this world that the world has been very ready to borrow from

Christianity when it has suited it to do so. It has rejected the doctrine, but it has often accepted the improved state of life. One thinks of a man like Mr. Ghandi who was avowedly not a Christian, but who was always ready to borrow Christian teaching when it suited him; and there are others who do the same thing. People who believe in other religions borrow from Christianity, and there have been improvements that have resulted in that way.

But that is not the whole of my answer. I suggest to you that the improvements of which we hear so much are general and superficial. Can we still go on boasting of improvements as we look at the state of the world in general? Do we still boast of progress in this twentieth century after our two world wars and all the uncertainty that characterises life; is that advance? Look at the state of society on a smaller scale. We say man is improving, but has there ever been so much selfishness manifested in the life of the nation as there is today, a self-centredness as well as a self-seeking? It is the only explanation of the appalling increase in divorce; it is the whole explanation of the spirit of greed; it is the whole basis of the attitude of the average person towards work—I do the minimum, I get the maximum—greed, self-centredness, the increasing rudeness in life, the increasing lack of consideration for others, the appalling suffering that is caused to innocent little children through the sheer selfishness of parents. The whole attitude towards life today as looked at in every respect is one that is showing this self-centredness. We do certain things on the surface, but man as man is still this selfish creature.

To put it finally, you see the truth of our doctrine most of all in the attitude of the world towards God. That is the ultimate way of testing the spirit of man or the spirit of the world. The devil, as we have seen, is one who hates God, and his primary concern is that God should be attacked and that the world should be kept from Him. The devil cares very little what men and women may be like, so long as they do not believe in God. It is not a question of culture, because people may be highly cultured and yet godless. This is where all of us are so polite when we look at things superficially and say the world is improving. The ultimate test is the attitude of men and women towards God, and in particular their attitude towards the Lord Jesus Christ. The final test is not how cultured or how polite they may be superficially, but whether they are still opposed to God; whether they hate God and do not believe on the Lord Jesus Christ. And I think that if we view it in that way, we will have to admit that the world is as much in the power of the evil one today as it has ever been. Some of the most educated men and women have been the most prominent in their hatred of God, in their scoffing at religion, in their ridicule of the supernatural and the miraculous, in their refusal to believe on the Lord Jesus Christ, and in their antagonism to the Cross and to the blood of Christ shed for man's sin. It is this that supremely proves that 'the whole world lieth in the wicked one.'

That, according to Scripture, is the view of life in this world. Men and women were made for God and were meant to serve God and enjoy Him; but they are in the grip of Satan. So they hate the name of God, and because of this they are unhappy. They are unhappy within themselves; they cannot find satisfaction; they are unhappy with other people because they blame them for their trouble. They do not say that it is in themselves—they are all little gods fighting with one another, jealous and envious of one another. That is the meaning of the state of the world according to the Bible. 'From whence come wars and fightings among you?' The answer is: 'Come they not hence, even of your lusts . . . ?' (Jas 4:1).

It is this enmity towards God, this failure to worship God and reverence Him, that is the problem. Those who are in the hands of Satan must be unhappy, and this is the meaning of everything in life. The life of men and women in this world, according to the Bible, is suicidal; they are destroying themselves and marring their own true destiny. They are as they are and behave as they do and their world is as it is because Satan is governing and controlling and keeping them from God, who is waiting to bless them. So here we are abounding in misery, overwhelmed by trouble, denying our God and refusing salvation and bliss with the Lord Jesus Christ. That is the biblical view of life in this world. The problem is not an 'evolutionary lag'; it is not economic or political problems; it is not a mere matter of education and knowledge and culture; it is not that we need to be taught higher morality or appealed to to be honest and kind. It is none of these things. The trouble is spiritual; men and women must be converted in their relationship to God, and they must see that they are in the grip of God's greatest enemy, who is blinding them and restraining them lest they should turn to God in repentance and worship Him and know Him and the Lord Jesus Christ, His Son, who has come even into the world to save it and who alone can conquer Satan.

Oh, may God grant us this increasing spiritual insight into the life of the world, that we may not only see it and flee from it and fight it, but above all that we may work without ceasing to deliver others out of it and to bring them to a knowledge of the glorious liberty of the children of God.

15

Of God

And we know that we are of God, and the whole world lieth in wickedness [the wicked one].

1 JOHN 5:19

We have found that if we are to come into this position into which John is so anxious that these people should come—namely, that we should be walking with God, experiencing this rich fellowship with Him and with His Son Jesus Christ, and rejoicing in the benefits of joy that result from it—then it is obviously essential that we should be very clear as to the condition and the state of this world in which we live. And it is still more important that we should know who we are and what we are and what the things are that are possible to us and for us as Christians and as children of God.

So we have looked at this definition of the world as something that 'lieth in the wicked one.' We have seen that the ultimate object of the devil is always to get us to turn away from God, and always to hold us in a kind of thraldom to this world and to ourselves—to do anything, in other words, that would distract our attention away from God, anything that would disturb our relationship and our fellowship with Him. 'The world,' we saw, is a very inclusive term; but it is ultimately anything that tries to make us feel satisfied without fellowship and communion with God.

That, then, is the world. Now let us look at what John has to tell us about Christians themselves—Christians' view of themselves in contra-distinction to their view of the world. And what John tells us about ourselves is this: '*we are of God.*' Surely we must at times be astounded at these laconic statements of the Scriptures. 'That is the whole truth about you,' says John, 'you are of God.' Now again I would remind you that the Apostle says that we 'know' this; we must know it—it is the essential thing that we are to grasp and understand; it is a confident affirmation. 'These three things,' says John, 'that I am here underlining for you are things about which there should be no doubt and no discussion. This is not something at which you hope to arrive; no, we are confident, we are assured, there is utter, absolute certainty about this—we *know* that we are of God.' This has been, as we have seen so repeatedly, the great theme of the entire epistle. That is the knowledge to which John was bringing them—'These things have I written unto you that believe on the name of the Son of God; that ye may know that ye have eternal life' (v 13). There it is, the same thing. So I ask once more, do we know this; are we able to say it?

What, then, does John mean by saying that 'we are of God'? Well, obviously it is a complete contrast to the other statement that 'the whole world lieth in the wicked one.' And it is not only a complete contrast to it—it is the only possible contrast. Here, in other words, we are once more looking at one of the great, characteristic New Testament definitions of the Christian; that is the great theme of the New Testament. Obviously Christians are not just good people, not even just moral people. Let us go further: Christians are not even just religious people. You can be good, you can be moral, you can even be religious and still not be a Christian. So John's definition of Christian men and women is not that they are benefactors, not even those who are highly moral and have noble ideas; not people who are religious and give their whole life to religion.

Christians are those who are '*of God*'; nothing less than that. So let
us start by some negative definitions of what John means.

To say that Christians are 'of God' means that they have been
taken out of the clutches of the wicked one. You notice that in dealing with this verse I have started with the end rather than with the
beginning: 'We know that we are of God, and the whole world lieth
in the wicked one.' I had a reason for that—it helps us to understand
what is meant by being 'of God.' We are all born in the world and
in the clutches of the wicked one; we are all born, as Paul puts it in
writing to the Ephesians, 'the children of wrath' (Eph 2:3); we are
all born in sin and shapen in iniquity (Psa 51:5). So we all start our
lives in this world 'in the wicked one,' in his grasp, belonging to that
kingdom of the devil and under his dominion. To be 'of God,' then,
obviously means that we are taken out of the clutches of sin; we are
no longer lying 'in the wicked one.'

Now the New Testament is fond of saying this. Paul, for
instance, in writing to the Galatians, bursts out at the beginning in
a hymn of praise as he mentions the name of the Lord Jesus Christ:
'who gave himself for our sins, that he might deliver us from this
present evil world' (Gal 1:4). That is it! We were in this present
world and in its chains and shackles, but Christ has offered Himself
and has died for us and thereby has delivered us. Or listen to Paul
again in writing to the Colossians: 'who hath delivered us,' he says,
'from the power of darkness, and hath translated us into the kingdom of his dear Son' (Col 1:13). That is simply a repetition of what
John is saying here. Everything, we have seen, is under the power
and the dominion of Satan; but now we have been moved, trans-
ferred into the kingdom of God's dear Son.

Or take another statement that Paul makes in writing to the
Romans when he says, 'Sin shall not have dominion over you'
(Rom 6:14). Why? Because you are taken out of his dominion. You
no longer belong to that realm; you are no longer citizens of such
a kingdom. The Apostle Peter says exactly the same thing: 'which
in time past were not a people, but are now the people of God;

which had not obtained mercy, but now have obtained mercy' (1 Pet 2:10). He has brought us, he says, 'out of darkness into his marvellous light' (1 Pet 2:9). All these are but different ways of expressing what John is saying here. So that to be 'of God' means negatively that we are no longer lying 'in the wicked one'; we have been brought out, emancipated, set free. Describe it as you will, it is a marvellous way of looking at it. And the negative is almost as good as the positive at this point. I say almost because it is not as good. But it is a great thing to know that we have been taken out of that kingdom and dominion.

What, then, does it mean positively to say that we are 'of God'? Well, we can sum it up by saying that we belong to God, to His realm, to His kingdom. This is a complete antithesis of everything that we saw in the other statement. But let us analyse it; it is such a rich statement that, in a sense, we cannot analyse it too much. It means, of necessity, that we must have been forgiven by Him, because as long as we belong to the realm and the dominion of Satan, we are enemies of God. Satan is the archenemy of God; he is everything that represents enmity against God, and all in his kingdom are enemies of God and under His wrath. So to be 'of God' means that we have been reconciled to God; we have come into an entirely new relationship to Him.

But it does not stop at that, of course, because it must mean also that we have received life from God. We are 'of God' in the sense that we are born of God, 'partakers of the divine nature,' as Peter says (2 Pet 1:4); we have received the life of God Himself. We are 'of God' in the sense that we have come out of God, and the life we now have is the life that is derived from Him. We are of God by the new birth. But it also means that our very existence and continuance is by God and of God; we not only receive this divine life once, but we go on receiving it. We are 'of God' in the sense that our whole being is dependent upon Him, that our sustenance, our everything, is derived from Him.

Let me, then, sum it up by saying, as I have already suggested, that it means that we belong to God and to the family of God. Have you thought of it in terms of 'party'? It means that we belong to God's party. We are no longer of the party of Satan and everything that represents; we now belong to God's party. We belong to God's family and are thus in this intimate relationship to Him. This is not merely an intellectual relationship; it is not even a faith one. It is more than that; we have become the children of God, and we belong to Him in that family sense.

But, of course, having said that, we must go on to say certain other things because John is always interested in the practical application. If we are 'of God' in that sense, it means also that we delight in God and we rejoice in Him. The natural man, the man who belongs to the world, does not delight in God; the natural man is, according to Paul, His enemy, and that is absolutely true. There are many people in this world who say they believe in God, but let something go wrong with them and they soon show how they are at enmity with Him. Indeed, the world would be very glad if someone could prove there is no God; that is its attitude. In the depths men and women do not delight in God; they do not rejoice in Him. But we are 'of God'; God is the centre not only of the universe, but of our whole life and outlook.

And that in turn must mean that we who are 'of God' are controlled by Him and by His Spirit. We have seen that those who are in the world and of the world are controlled by Satan and are governed by him; that is the terrible part of that life. Our Lord put it in a terrifying picture when He said, 'When a strong man armed keepeth his palace, his goods are in peace' (Luke 11:21). There is a terrible kind of peace under the dominion of Satan. It is the peace of men and women who are not allowed to do anything. They are hemmed in; they are held there. Why don't people believe the gospel? asks Paul in writing his second letter to the Corinthians. And the answer is this: 'The god of this world hath blinded the minds of them which believe not' (4:4). They cannot believe. The devil is preventing them; he is controlling them. But Christians,

who do believe, are opposite to that. They are 'of God'; they are
directed and governed by God.

And that in turn comes to this, that they are people who are living for God; it is their desire to live for Him. Let me put it like this:
we saw, in considering the case of those who belong to the world,
that ultimately it comes right back to slavery; the devil holds men
and women in his own grasp by persuading them that it is to their
own best and highest interest. The principle that is governing the
world is self-centredness, selfishness, and self-seeking; to be of God,
therefore, obviously means that we no longer live for self or Satan,
but we live for God, and our supreme desire is to please Him. We
are 'of God.' That is our party; that is our interest. He is our Father.
As Philip Doddridge wrote:

> 'Tis to my Saviour I would live,
> To Him who for my ransom died.

Ah yes, but it must mean also that if I am 'of God,' in the sense
that I am born of Him and am a partaker of the divine nature, there
must be some signs of this in my life. The New Testament is always
very careful to press this and to press it very strongly. As John
reminds us in the first chapter, 'If we say that we have fellowship
with him, and walk in darkness'—what is the truth about us? Well,
we are liars, says John; 'we lie, and do not the truth' (v 6). It is no
use saying you are 'of God' and then showing that you live under
the dominion of Satan, in the life of Satan as it were. That would
be a contradiction, a lie; if we are 'of God,' we must have certain
manifestations to the effect that the life of God is in us. What are
these? We have repeatedly reminded one another of them as we
worked our way through this epistle. The tests that John applies
are: keeping His commandments; loving the brethren; believing the
truth about the Lord Jesus Christ; these are the tests of life.

Or if you like, you can state this in terms of what the Apostle
Paul calls 'the fruit of the Spirit.' In other words, if the Spirit is in

you, if the life of God is in you, certain fruits will begin to appear.
What are they? 'Love, joy, peace, longsuffering, gentleness, good-
ness, faith, meekness, temperance' (Gal 5:22-23). This is inevitable,
and the great teachers of the Church throughout the ages have generally emphasised that one of the most important and vital tests is
the test of humility. The great St. Augustine said that the first test
of the Christian life, and the second, and the third is humility. 'Be
clothed with humility,' says Peter (1 Pet 5:5), and that must be the
test because there is nothing that stands out more gloriously in the
life of our blessed Lord Himself than just that. Though He was God
and equal with God, He thought it not something to be clutched
at; He humbled Himself. 'Let this mind be in you also,' says Paul
(Phil 2:5); 'who,' says Peter, 'when he was reviled, reviled not again;
when he suffered, he threatened not; but committed himself to him
that judgeth righteously' (1 Pet 2:23).

This must be the ultimate test because the worldly spirit is the
very antithesis of this—pride, arrogance, self-confidence, and assurance. The world is full of it. Look at your newspapers—it is there
shouting at you. The worldly are always praising us, making us
believe we are wonderful. And look at men and women in their
speeches. Listen to them—the self that is being manifested. In its psychological training the world would encourage you to rely upon
yourself, to believe in yourself. It says that nothing is impossible if
you believe in yourself; always self—that is the spirit of the world.
The world, in a sense, knew nothing about true humility until
Christ came into it. That is the ultimate test. We show signs of His
life in us in that way, and one of the most delicate and subtle tests
is just this test of humility, the very antithesis of everything that the
world represents and stands for.

But the last way in which I define this being 'of God' is that we
are destined for God. We are returning to God; we are making our
way to Him. We are going to eternity with Him and shall spend it
in His presence. I like to think that Christians, in a sense, are men
and women who have a label on them; their destination is booked,

they are marked. They are 'of God,' and they are for God. They are going to God; they have a new name written upon them, and it is *God.* They are God's property; you and I are 'of God' in that sense. 'The whole world lieth in the wicked one'; it is the devil's property, his luggage, and it is destined for destruction and perdition. It is destined for the lake of fire that burns without ceasing for ever and ever; that is its destiny–that is the destiny of the devil, and it goes with him. But we are 'of God.' We are destined for God; we are meant for Him. We belong to God, and we shall spend eternity with Him.

That, then, is something of what the New Testament teaching means by the use of this term 'of God.' But remember, we say that Christians realise this is all true of them not as a result of anything they are, not as a result of anything they have done, but entirely and solely as the result of the grace of the Lord Jesus Christ, because of His coming into this world and the perfect work that He has accomplished for us. We are 'of God' because He has bought us and ransomed us and delivered us by taking hold of us and translating us into His own kingdom.

So we can see that the way in which we read a verse like this is of vital importance. I started by saying that there are many people who dislike this sort of statement and feel that it suggests an arrogance if we say, 'We are of God, and the whole world lieth in the wicked one.' They say that suggests a kind of censorious spirit, a lack of charity with regard to those who are not Christians. But I hope that nobody feels like that about this statement now. We have looked at what it means to be 'in the wicked one,' and we have considered what it means to be 'of God.' How does one say this? Well, there is no arrogance or pride or boasting. The people who say this truly, as we have seen, are those who say it with a deep and profound sense of gratitude; it is all of Christ. We were hell-deserving sinners and were destined for it; but Christ has saved and rescued us, and we say it with a sense of wonder.

I believe increasingly that the most delicate test we can ever have of the fact that we are Christians is that we are amazed and surprised at that fact, that we never cease to wonder at ourselves. We have a sense of escape, of having been delivered. We have a deep consciousness of the privilege and a consciousness of the responsibility. We look at ourselves and say, 'Am I of God in that sense? Is that true of me? Is it possible that I am going to be with Him and in His presence for all eternity? Is it possible that such a worm as I should be able to say, "Abba Father" and know that the eternal everlasting God is my Father in the Lord Jesus Christ?' We are 'of God'–oh, the wonder and amazement of it all, the surprise and the gratitude, the praise and the thanksgiving, the privilege and the high responsibility! That is the way such a statement is to be said.

But let me go further and say that if you cannot say this and if you feel that objection to saying this, it is because your idea of a Christian is wrong. The people who do not like this statement are those who think that they are Christians because of what they do; and then it would indeed be boasting. If I say it because I am such a wonderful man or woman, that is the height of pride and arrogance. But if I say it like this: 'By the grace of God I am what I am' (1 Cor 15:10) and 'there but for the grace of God go I,' then there is no pride. Arrogance and boastfulness are removed because we realise that we are what we are solely because of God's wondrous love and His amazing grace in the Lord Jesus Christ.

What, then, are the views of Christian people in the light of these two definitions?

Well, in general we see that the world is not something that is gradually improving. Indeed, we go further and say that the world cannot be improved in an ultimate sense. In the last analysis, any hope of this world ever being improved or reformed or Christianised is nothing but a simple denial of the most essential and primary New Testament message. Anything that 'lieth in the wicked one' can never be improved ultimately.

But wait a minute! I have not finished my statement–that is

only the first step. My second is that all the same, evil must be controlled and kept within bounds. The world cannot be improved in an ultimate sense, but that does not mean that we do not do our utmost to control evil and its manifestations and its effects in it. It is God's world, and God has appointed kings and governments and magistrates, according to the Scriptures, so that evil and its effects may be kept within bounds and a limit put upon them. The forty-fifth chapter of the prophecy of Isaiah makes the statement that God said, 'I create evil' (v 7), which in one sense means that He controls it. He has it within His grasp, and it will not be allowed to proceed beyond a certain limit.

Then my third step is that evil is something that will finally be judged and damned. 'Love not the world,' says John in this epistle, 'neither the things that are in the world.' Why? 'The world passeth away, and the lust thereof' (2:15, 17). The world is doomed; judgment is coming for certain. History is working up to a grand climax, and the climax will be the return of Christ and the judgement of the world in this particular spiritual sense. Satan and all who belong to him will be finally condemned and destroyed. The world as we know it, without God and without Christ, is but awaiting the end that is surely coming. If reform were possible, reform would take place; but there is no ultimate reform—the world will be destroyed.

That is the view of the world in general. But what about people who are in the world? Well, the Christian's view of the people in the world is that we must regard them as being in a desperate and dangerous position. They belong to a kingdom that is already doomed and will be condemned and destroyed, and they need to be rescued. They need to be delivered, to be emancipated. We know they can be, and that is the whole point in preaching the gospel. We know that 'we are of God, and the whole world lieth in the wicked one'; it lies in him, but it can be brought out of him! We were all there to start with, but we have been taken out. We are now 'of God,' so that our view of those who are in this world and who belong to it is that they are in this dangerous condition, and our hearts should be filled with compassion. We should have great concern and anxiety, and we should be doing everything we can to bring them out of that dominion. We should tell them of the gospel and show them the Redeemer, that they may be brought from that position in the wicked one and be translated into the kingdom of God and of His dear Son. That is our view of people in the world.

Lastly, what is our view of ourselves, as we still live and exist in this world? Well, here is the New Testament teaching: the world is something that is actively hostile to us in a most subtle manner; it is doing its utmost to separate us from God. That is Satan's whole object and intention. He is 'the accuser of our brethren' (Rev 12:10); he is the adversary of our souls. The world we are living in is something that is extremely dangerous to us, something that is all the time trying to infiltrate us. It is always making suggestions to us; it suggests that its life is a larger and a bigger and a freer life—the subtle antagonism of the world to us—the flesh warring against the spirit.

So we can say that the world in its spirit is a thing that we are to avoid. 'Pure religion and undefiled before God and the Father is this, To visit the fatherless and widows in their affliction, and to keep himself unspotted from the world' (Jas 1:27). Never forget that; it is a great statement. You have to work in this world, but while you are doing that, you must be careful to keep yourself unspotted from it. Jude in his epistle says the same thing, that we must save those who have gone back into sin but watch ourselves so that our garments do not become spotted by that evil (v 23). The world is something to be avoided; we must do everything we can to restrain evil. The Christian is a citizen in this world; but let us be careful that the world does not enter into us again and get us back. We are to avoid this spirit of the world.

The last thing, therefore, is this: the world is something from which we are constantly needing to be cleansed. As we walk in it and thus are actively busy in it, we constantly become defiled by it, and we need constant cleansing from the stain of the world and its sin. But thank God, the provision is perfect. John, you remember, has told us that in the first chapter: 'If we walk in the light, as he is in the light, we have fellowship one with another, and the blood of Jesus Christ his Son cleanseth us from all sin. . . . If we confess our sins, he is faithful and just to forgive us our sins, and to cleanse us from all unrighteousness' (vv 7, 9). The defilement is there, and the sin; but, my dear friend, do not be depressed. Immediately confess the sin, and acknowledge it, and ask God to cleanse you again and renew you; He has promised to do so. 'If any man sin, we have an advocate with the Father, Jesus Christ the righteous: and he is the propitiation for our sins: and not for ours only, but also for the sins of the whole world' (1 John 2:2).

What a tremendous statement that is, and how important! You and I are 'of God,' strangers and pilgrims in this world—a colony of heaven, says Paul to the Philippians, and we are far from home. But we are going towards home in an alien land, and we have to remember that and bear it in mind. 'We are of God, and the whole world lieth in the wicked one.' Let us have a right view of the world; let us have a right view of its history; let us understand what is happening to the world at this present time; let us look ahead and see what it is destined for; let us never rest our affection on it. And as we go on, let us remember its subtle insinuations, and let us beware of its defilement and sin. But let us ever remember that whenever we may fall or be conscious of defilement, the blood of Christ still avails; we can be washed, we can be cleansed anew. We can continue to walk in blessed fellowship with the Father and with His Son, Jesus Christ. 'We are of God'—amazing! But 'the whole world lieth in the wicked one,' so let us have pity, mercy, and compassion upon others and tell them of the way of escape.

16

Understanding

And we know that the Son of God is come, and hath given
us an understanding, that we may know him that is true;
and we are in him that is true, even in his Son Jesus Christ.
This is the true God, and eternal life.

1 JOHN 5:20

T his is the third and the last of the three confident affirmations that we find here in the postscript to this first epistle
of John. It is interesting to observe the sequence that was
obviously in the Apostle's mind as he uttered these three affirmations. His main concern is, of course, the whole problem of sin and
evil. This is the great theme of the entire Bible; how are men and
women to live in this world in a godly manner and in a manner that
is well-pleasing in God's sight? That is the great problem of life and
existence according to the Bible. Its view of life, as we have seen
repeatedly, is a spiritual view; and so this is especially the question
that should be uppermost in the minds of all those who call themselves Christian.

Now John has been giving these great assurances that those
who are born of God do not continue in a state of sin, that being
'of God' and having been translated from the kingdom of Satan into
the kingdom of God's dear Son we are in this unique and separate

position. But he still feels that something else is necessary, and that is what we have in this twentieth verse. He is still thinking in terms of the world that is around and about us and of that wicked one, that evil power that is set against us; that is our problem, and we must never lose sight of it. Our life in this world is a spiritual warfare, whether we want it or not; it is inevitably so, because of Satan.

You see that clearly in the life of the Son of God Himself, how constantly He was attacked and besieged by Satan. Satan only left Him for a season after the temptation in the wilderness; then he came back. Because Satan is the god of this world and governs and orders it, the whole life of the Christian is, of necessity, one of spiritual conflict. Yet John has reminded us, as we have seen, of certain things that are a great comfort and consolation to us, and now here is the last of these, one which is a great comfort. It is that we have an '*understanding*', that we are able to see this thing.

The tragedy of those who are not Christians is that they are not only blinded by sin, but that they are unaware of that fact. That, according to the Bible, is the real tragedy of mankind when it is not in relationship to God. It goes through life in this world and persuades itself that all is well, that it is fairly happy, not realising the terrible doom that is awaiting it. It lacks an understanding; it does not know. Before one can ever wage a successful warfare against these powers of evil and darkness that are around and about us, we must be aware of their existence. We must know something about them, and we must know some of the resources that are available for those who are anxious to overcome them. And here, says John, is something again that we know and for which we can thank God: 'We know that the Son of God is come, and hath given us an understanding, that we may know him that is true.' We are able to differentiate between the truth and lies, between light and darkness; not only are we not in the clutches of Satan, but we know God, we are 'of God,' and we belong to Him. We are in Him and in His Son, Jesus Christ.

That, then, is the connection between these three confident

affirmations that are made here by the Apostle; and, surely, we must agree with him that nothing is more important than that we should know these three things for certain. So let us concentrate now upon what it is that enables us to know them. We do not 'think'; we are not on the whole persuaded or have some misgivings or are nearly sure. No; *we 'know'*! The Christian position is one of certainty—no doubt, no hesitation; it is a clear-cut position. This is something, as we have already considered, that you find running through the Bible. There is this great division going on from beginning to end—Noah and his family in the ark, the rest of the world outside; God's people and those who are not God's people. And the great characteristic of the people of God is that they 'know' certain things.

That, of course, is the whole secret of their life; that is the argument, for instance, of that great eleventh chapter of Hebrews concerning the heroes of the faith. Why was it that those men and women behaved as they did? What made Abraham leave his country and go out? What was it that made Moses, who had the prospect of being adopted by the daughter of Pharaoh, with a wonderful career before him in the court of Egypt—what made him reject it all and become a mere shepherd and endure the adversity that he experienced for so long? What was the secret of all those people? Well, according to the writer of the epistle to the Hebrews, it was just that they knew certain things. They had their eye on 'the recompense of the reward' (v 26); they had a particular view of this world and of life in this world, and therefore they preferred 'to suffer affliction with the people of God, than to enjoy the pleasures of sin for a season' (v 25). And that is the great case of the Bible everywhere.

Now there are so many things in the modern world that ought to enable us men and women in this generation to see these things with a particular clarity. In many ways I thank God that I am preaching this gospel now rather than in the nineteenth century, and I say that because though I know it was then the popular thing for people to go to a place of worship—Christianity was, in a sense, fashionable and it paid to be a Christian—in spite of all that, it seems to me that it was more difficult to see the true nature of life in this world then than it is now. People harboured those great illusions about a perpetual state of peace and prosperity and progress and development. There had not been a war of any magnitude since the Napoleonic, and they had great confidence and optimism. They seemed to have lost sight of the fact that Satan is the god of this world and that you cannot by human effort and endeavour produce a perfect society in a world like this while sin is sin and men and women are governed by sin.

But today that should be painfully obvious to all of us with the things that we have experienced in this century. Surely we of all people ought to be seeing so clearly that we are surrounded by evil powers and forces that the one thing that should be concerning us is, what can we do in a world like this? How can we master and conquer it; how can we avoid being engulfed in the vortex and being drowned in this terrible world? Well, the answer is to be found here in this one verse, and it obviously has a very direct reference to what happened at Pentecost.[1] The whole secret is that we may have 'an understanding,' and the message is that 'the Son of God is come, and hath given us an understanding,' so that we may have a right view of all these things.

In other words, this reference to the 'understanding' in this text is nothing but a very direct piece of teaching with regard to the Holy Spirit. For what John says is that the Son of God has come and has done something to our minds. He has not merely come and revealed and displayed the Father to us and told us certain things about Him. No; He has done something more than that, something that, in a sense, is even more vital than that: He has enabled us to understand these things. 'Understanding' means the mind, the depth of the mind, that rational part of our being that enables us to grasp the truth; and, therefore, it is clearly a reference to the work of the Holy Spirit and what He enables us to do.

The first thing, therefore, that we can lay down is that the Holy

Spirit is the gift of Jesus Christ. 'We know,' says John, 'that the Son of God is come, and hath given us an understanding.' Now this is something of supreme importance. Whit-Sunday, this day on which we remember together what happened at Jerusalem on that great Day of Pentecost, is of vital importance in Christian doctrine and in an understanding of the Christian truth. We must always be clear and certain as to what took place on that occasion. There, as was expounded by the Apostle Peter, something happened that had long been promised by God. 'Therefore,' he says, 'being by the right hand of God exalted, and having received of the Father the promise of the Holy Ghost, he hath shed forth this, which ye now see and hear' (Acts 2:33). 'What has happened today,' said Peter in effect to that assembled concourse, 'is nothing but a fulfilment of the prophecy that you find in the Old Testament.' He had already put it in terms of the fulfilment of the prophecy according to Joel.

In other words, the ultimate purpose of the coming of the Lord Jesus Christ into this world was to send this gift of the Holy Spirit upon His people. Must we not agree that there is a tendency for us to forget that? Is there not a tendency on our part to stop with the life and example and teaching of Jesus Christ, or to stop only with His work upon the cross, as if to say that the whole purpose of the coming of the Son of God into this world was to purchase pardon and forgiveness for us and nothing more? Thank God that we do emphasise that, and it is ever central, and must be; but the work of the Lord Jesus Christ does not end at that point. His work in the resurrection is equally vital for us; His ascension, too, is equally important; and, above all, this great event that took place on the Day of Pentecost at Jerusalem.

The way in which the Bible puts it is this: what people needed was a new spirit; they needed this new relationship to God, this understanding that could only be given to them by God. And running through the Old Testament there is a promise of this. There is a contrast between the giving of the law through Moses and this further new understanding that was to be given. The law was given by Moses on stones; it was given externally. The law was given to men and women, and they were told to read that law and try to put it into practice, 'which if a man do, he shall live in them,' said God (Lev 18:5). But the prophecy was that a day would come when God would make a new covenant with men and women. He would write His law in their minds and place it in their hearts. The law would no longer be something external; it would be something that would be put right into them, into their very essence. So they would no longer look at the law and painfully try to keep it and fail. They would want to keep it, they would love to keep it; it would be something working within them. That was the great promise; that was something to which the people of God looked forward. So the New Testament refers to it as 'the promise of the Father' (Acts 1:4).

Now this was what the world needed, and according to this Scripture, Jesus Christ, having come into the world, has made that possible. He came into the world; the Son of God became incarnate. He took upon Himself the form of man and the likeness of sinful flesh, and the Holy Spirit was given to Him in all His fulness. Look at Him and watch His life, and you will see that there was never a life like this. He was free from sin; He was able to master and to conquer Satan. He had unusual powers that enabled Him to control the elements of nature and to work His wonderful miracles. It is a life apart, and it is a life that is to be explained, according to the Scripture, in terms of the Holy Spirit. Though He was the Son of God, He humbled Himself; He did not make use of the prerogatives of His Godhead. That is the meaning of His self-humbling, that He lived life as a man; He was given the gift of the Holy Spirit, and He depended upon Him, and this is the result. As we look at that life, we say, 'Oh that we could live such a life! Oh, that it were possible for us to live in that way!'

And the answer of the Bible to us is that it is possible; that He, having come thus into the world and having rendered perfect obedience to God's law, went even to the death of the cross. There He made Himself responsible for our guilt and for our sin; the thing that stood between mankind and God was there removed. He has thus, by dying upon the cross, purchased our pardon; He has made Himself our Redeemer and Rescuer. Then He ascended into heaven and presented Himself and His perfect offering; He presented His own blood as an expiation for all sin, and God received Him. And—this is the wonderful sequence—because of what He has done, God has given to Him the gift of the Holy Spirit to give us. By dying thus, Peter argued on the Day of Pentecost, exalted by God, He has received 'the promise of the Father.' God, as it were, rewarded Him for the work He had done for mankind by giving Him this gift of the Holy Spirit to give to us, and there on that Day of Pentecost at Jerusalem He showered forth this gift that He had received from the Father.

'You cannot understand it,' says Peter to that assembled concourse in Jerusalem; 'you are amazed at the fact that we are able to speak in other tongues. Some of you have suggested we are drunk, but that is impossible because it is only the third hour of the day. You are bewildered and amazed by what you see, and you ask, What is this that you are doing, what is this power? Well,' says Peter, 'this is just the fulfilment of prophecy. Jesus of Nazareth, whom you crucified, is none other than the only begotten Son of God. He, by doing what He has done, has become the Prince and Saviour of Israel. God has given Him this gift, and He has showered it forth upon us. That is why we are what we are. This is that which was spoken of by the prophet Joel; this is the promise of the Father.' Therefore, what happened on the Day of Pentecost at Jerusalem is nothing but a fulfilment of those ancient prophecies—that prophecy of Joel, that prophecy of Jeremiah about the new covenant and about the writing of the laws in the mind and upon the heart (Jeremiah 31:31-34).

Indeed, this is the perfect fulfilment of that which we find in John 7:39. Our Lord said to the people in Jerusalem, 'If any man thirst, let him come unto me, and drink' (v 37). 'If there is anybody amongst you,' says Christ in effect, 'who is conscious of weakness and tiredness, if there is anybody who has been battling against sin and is conscious of defeat, if there is any man who needs a power that will enable him to overcome, let him come unto me and drink. And,' He said, 'if he does so, from his inward parts shall flow rivers of living water (v 38). He will not simply be filled—he will overflow; this great power will come upon him from Me; if he is thirsty and drinks of Me, that will be the result.' Then says John in recording all this, 'this spake he of the Spirit, which they that believe on him should receive; for the Holy Ghost was not yet given' (v 39). Christ, says John, was speaking at that point of what the Holy Spirit was going to do when He would come; and on the Day of Pentecost at Jerusalem, that very thing happened. He poured forth His Holy Spirit upon the assembled church.

There were one hundred and twenty people in the upper room waiting. He had told them to do that, and He had said, 'I will pour out my Spirit upon you, and then you will be My witnesses. You cannot do it without this gift.' And the gift came, they began to witness, and prophecy was fulfilled. So the Holy Spirit is the gift of the Lord Jesus Christ. You remember how, even before the Day of Pentecost, when He appeared to the disciples in the upper room, we are told that He breathed upon them and said, 'Receive ye the Holy Ghost' (John 20:22) He gives us the Spirit; the Spirit is the gift of the Father to the Son as the triumphant mediator, the Redeemer and Saviour, and He in turn gives the Spirit to His people. 'We know,' says John, 'that the Son of God is come, and hath given us this gift of the Holy Spirit.'

That, then, leads to the second principle, that it is through this gift of the Holy Spirit alone that we have or can have any spiritual knowledge and 'understanding.' This, of course, is obviously the central doctrine in these matters. What we need is understanding. If the world is, as the Bible tells us, under the control of Satan, and if we are all helpless face-to-face with Satan, the one thing we need is knowledge and enlightenment. And according to the Scripture, that is only possible as we receive the gift of the Holy Ghost. The trouble with the world apart from the Holy Spirit is that, as Paul puts it in writing to the Ephesians, non-Christians are living 'in the vanity of their mind, having the understanding darkened' (Eph 4:17-18). There is a kind of shutter that has come down on their minds. As we have seen, the god of this world has blinded them, as Paul says in writing to the Corinthians; the world by nature lacks a spiritual faculty and understanding.

Now surely we all must recognise the importance of this. Let me put it in this way: Are you surprised at the state of the world or of society? Does it come to you sometimes with astonishment that the world is as it is, that men and women can be so carefree? Is it not a remarkable thing that, having had two world wars and all the continuing uncertainty in the world, our newspapers can be filled with trivial things? Does it not seem incredible? And yet that is a fact. How do you explain that in the face of many tragic possibilities the world can laugh and joke and enjoy itself and be apparently carefree; what is the explanation?

There is only one adequate explanation. It is that the world's understanding is darkened. It does not see what is happening; it is not aware of the tragedy. This is only possible because the minds of men and women are blinded, and that is precisely what the Bible says about them. The trouble with people in this world is that they are fooled by Satan. Satan persuades them, 'Eat, drink and be merry, for tomorrow you die. What is the use of worrying about any possible catastrophe? All the worry in the world will not affect it; it will come soon enough without going to meet it. So have a good time; turn your back upon it!' That is the philosophy of the devil that the world believes; that is the tragic condition, and nothing will awaken men and women out of this but this enlightenment that comes alone by the Holy Spirit. We have received 'an understanding,' and our minds are awakened because the Son of God has come and has given us the gift of the Spirit.

You find this everywhere in Scripture. Take, for instance, the account of the Apostle Paul preaching for the first time in Europe.

Is it not interesting to observe what we are told about the first convert to Christianity? She was a woman named Lydia living in a place called Philippi. The Apostle Paul went there to preach the gospel, she and others listened to him, and she believed the things that were told her. She came to see that you must believe and accept the gospel and give yourself to it, and her life was transformed by it. And the Scripture says that it happened because the Lord 'opened' her heart, that she might believe (Acts 16:14). If the Lord, through the Holy Spirit, had not opened her heart she would never have believed, for what the Holy Spirit does is to enlighten our spiritual faculty. He awakens certain things that are dormant in us and makes us understand.

Again, take the case of Nicodemus. He was a man who was a master in Israel, a teacher of the people. Here was a man of great reputation, a man of erudition and learning, a man who was an expert in the Old Testament and a teacher of the people in these matters. But having looked at Jesus Christ and having watched Him and having seen His miracles, he felt that here was someone whom he could not understand, someone who had a power greater than he or any other teacher in Israel had. And so he went one night and sought an interview with Jesus. He said to Him, 'Master, You must be a teacher sent from God, for no man could do the things that You do except God be with Him.' And immediately our Lord interrupted him and said, 'Verily, verily, I say unto thee, Except a man be born again, he cannot see the kingdom of God.' Poor Nicodemus began to expostulate, and our Lord replied again, 'Except a man be born of water and of the Spirit, he cannot enter into the kingdom of God' (John 3:2-5).

What does that mean? It means this: Nicodemus was trying to understand these things, and our Lord said to him in effect, 'My dear man, you cannot understand them. You are a master in Israel, but you must be born of the Spirit. You have to have this enlightenment that the Holy Ghost alone can give. You cannot advance

from Judaism to Christianity; you must be born again. You need a
new faculty, as it were, and the Holy Ghost alone can give it.'

'The wind,' said our Lord, 'bloweth where it listeth, and thou
hearest the sound thereof, but canst not tell whence it cometh, and
whither it goeth: so is every one that is born of the Spirit' (John
3:8). 'You must have this gift of God,' He said, 'and then, and then
only, will you understand these things.'

And the Apostle Paul has put this more explicitly still in writing
to the Corinthians. It is only the man who is spiritual, he says, who
can understand these things. When Christ, the Prince of Glory, was
here, said Paul, the princes of this world did not know him, for had
they known Him, 'they would not have crucified the Lord of glory.'
But we know Him because God has given us His Spirit, and 'the
Spirit searcheth all things, yea, the deep things of God' (1 Cor 2:8,
10). Only men and women of understanding know the things of the
Spirit of God because they have to be spiritually understood, and
the others lack that faculty. 'We have received, not the spirit of the
world, but the Spirit which is of God; that we might know the things
that are freely given to us of God' (1 Cor 2:12). It is only the Holy
Spirit who can give us this understanding.

But, says the Apostle John here, 'we know that the Son of God
is come, and hath given us an understanding.' He has given us the
gift of the Spirit. Now John has already emphasised this, you
remember, in the second chapter, where he says, 'Ye have an unction from the Holy One, and ye know all things. . . . But the anointing which ye have received of him abideth in you, and ye need not
that any man teach you: but as the same anointing teacheth you of
all things, and is truth, and is no lie, and even as it hath taught you,
ye shall abide in him' (vv 20, 27).

This is the great teaching throughout the Bible. It was only as
they were enlightened by the Spirit of God that those people of the
Old Testament understood the truth as they did. Look at those
prophets of Israel who not only prophesied to their own generation,
but who predicted things that were coming, who told of the com-

ing of Christ, where He would be born, and all these things–how did they do it? Peter answers that by telling us that 'no prophecy of the Scripture is of any private interpretation.' He says that these men did not write these things because they thought them out or because they suddenly got an idea from their own reasoning. Not at all! 'Holy men of God spake as they were moved [carried along, enlightened] by the Holy Ghost' (2 Pet 1:20-21). The Holy Spirit came in that way; the power of the Holy Spirit enlightened their understanding and guided them how to write. And the same thing is always true. It is only as we receive this gift of the Spirit that we shall understand; without that we remain in spiritual darkness. We are dead in trespasses and sins; we need to be quickened, enlightened in power and understanding, and then, and then alone, we have true spiritual knowledge.

And that brings us to the last word–what is this knowledge? Well, John summarises it once more, and I need only to give you headings therefore. The first thing that the Holy Spirit enables us to see and understand is the fact concerning Christ Himself. The world is not interested in Him and would explain Him away as a man; it is only those who have this spiritual understanding that know Him to be the Son of God, the Saviour of the world. Indeed they not only know things about Him–they know Him. 'We . . . know him,' says John.

And the same is true of God the Father. 'We know that the Son of God is come, and hath given us an understanding, that we may know him that is true'–that is, God the Father. Again, we not only know things about God–we know God. That is what John is emphasising. The Jews knew about God; the Mohammedan also knows things about God. But 'we . . . know him that is true.' We know Him as Father; we are in this relationship to Him. We have that knowledge of Him that enables us to cry out, 'Abba Father'; and this makes our prayer possible. But we not only know God– we know also that we are in God; and not only are we in God, but in His Son Jesus Christ also.

In other words, here at the end of the epistle John comes back to the thing with which he started. He started off, you remember, by saying that he is anxious that these people to whom he is writing may share in that fellowship that he and the Apostles are enjoying. 'Truly,' he says, 'our fellowship is with the Father, and with His Son Jesus Christ.' And the way that is made possible, he says, is: 'That which was from the beginning, which we have heard, which we have seen with our eyes, which we have looked upon, and our hands have handled, of the Word of life; (For the life was manifested, and we have seen it, and bear witness, and shew unto you that eternal life, which was with the Father, and was manifested unto us)' (1 John 1:1-3). He has come and has given us life, says John; and here he ends on exactly the same note. For by giving us the Holy Spirit, he has not only given us the faculty and understanding and the knowledge, but He has given us life itself. We are in Christ and in God, and God and Christ are in us.

If you read chapters 14, 15, and 16 of John's Gospel, you will find that there our Lord promises all that. He said to those people, 'I would tell you more, but you cannot bear it now. But after I have gone, I will send the gift of the Holy Spirit, and He will lead you into all truth—He will remind you of the things I have spoken unto you. Not only that, He will come and dwell in you, and He will be with you; and the Father will come, and the Father and I will make our abode with you, you in us and We in you.' Those are the essential things we are promised, so that even in this world we are given this 'understanding' by the Holy Spirit.

As Christian people we are not fooled by the world and its gaudy prizes; we are not for a moment misled by its supposed happiness, which we know is utterly artificial. We have been given 'an understanding'; we know something about the nature of sin in us and in the world around and about us. We have been given a knowledge of God and a relationship with Him; we have been given a knowledge concerning Christ as our Redeemer and Saviour; we have been given life by Him, so that we are in fellowship with God. We see the truth in contrast to evil; we are aware of that which is eternal in contra-distinction to the temporal. And being in God and in His Son Jesus Christ, we have a power, a might, and a strength that are more than enough to conquer Satan, so that we can look at the world and all its evil without fear. 'We know that the Son of God is come, and hath given us an understanding, that we may know him that is true. This [the Son] is the true God, and eternal life'; and having Him and knowing Him, we need have no fear. Thank God for the gift of the Holy Spirit; thank God for that which happened on the Day of Pentecost.

Have you this understanding; are you clear about your life in this world and of the victory that is possible to you? Have you this unction, this anointing about which the Apostle speaks; have you received the Holy Spirit? Those are the questions. If you have, you have nothing to do but to praise God and to yield yourself increasingly to Him and to ask that you may be filled with His Spirit more and more. If not, I repeat to you the word of the Lord Jesus Christ Himself: 'If ye then, being evil, know how to give good gifts unto your children; how much more shall your heavenly Father give the Holy Spirit to them that ask him' (Luke 11:13). We have but to ask, to seek, to knock and we shall receive. It is God's desire that we receive this gift; therefore, if we feel we lack the understanding, if we lack the power, if we lack the joy and happiness and the peace and the abounding life that the Holy Ghost gives, we have but to go to God in simplicity. We have but to confess our need and lack and ask Him for the gift of the Holy Spirit, and He is pledged to answer and to give us the gift. And having received the Holy Spirit, we shall have this understanding and begin to produce the fruit of the Spirit in our daily lives.

17

Idolatry

Little children, keep yourselves from idols. Amen.

1 JOHN 5:21

We thus once more and for the last time in this series consider the message of the first Epistle of John. For those who may be interested in statistics, it is actually the sixty-seventh time[1] that we have looked at this epistle together; and now here are the last words. They are John's final advice, his final warning to these people whom he loved so truly and whom he constantly addressed as 'little children.' That does not mean, you remember, that they were literally little children because, as we saw in the second chapter, he addresses them in different categories—'little children,' 'young men,' and 'fathers.' But it is his custom to use this term of endearment with regard to the whole body of people, and this is what he does here.

There are authorities who would say that these are probably the last words in the entire Scripture, if you take Scripture in chronological order. This point cannot be proved, but there is a good deal to be said for it. In any case, these are the last words of this old man who was so concerned about the life and the future of these Christians to whom he was writing. The words of an old man are always worthy of respect and consideration; they are words that are based upon a long lifetime's experience. The last words of all people are important, but the last words of great people are of exceptional importance, and the last words of an Apostle of the Lord Jesus Christ are of supreme importance.

So here we have this Apostle looking back across a long life, having had many and varied and strange experiences himself, a man who has looked back at a wonderful three years spent in the actual presence and company of the Son of God, who heard all His addresses, who saw His miracles and was with Him on every special occasion. Here is a man out of this great and mighty experience saying a last word. He is an old man; he knows the end is at hand, and he sees this group of people in a hostile world, and he wants them to live a life of victory. He wants them to have a joy that may be full, and this is his final word to them: 'Little children, keep yourselves from idols.'

Now in ending on this note John is doing something that is very characteristic of himself. We have seen repeatedly, as we have gone through this epistle together, his liking for contrast. He is very fond of comparing—light and darkness, love and hate, that which is true and that which is false. His mind instinctively seems to think in terms of these great contrasts, and he ends on that. The previous verse has told us that 'we know that the Son of God is come, and hath given us an understanding, that we may know him that is true; and we are in him that is true, even in His Son Jesus Christ. This is the true God, and eternal life.' Then he adds, 'Little children, keep yourselves from idols'—the false; this is a contrast between the true and the false.

Or we can put it like this: John was also very fond of negatives; he never contented himself with the positive only. So he generally puts his positive first and then his negative, and this is what he does here. We are not only told that we must keep the commandments and be perfect; we are also told that we must not sin. Here we see the negative in relation to the one and only true and living God—the avoidance of idols.

Or to put it yet another way, John always warns us. Now most people do not like warnings, and we instinctively do not like them, because we are sinners. We do not like to be told not to do something; we always feel that this is insulting because it proves that we need the warning. But John, out of his long experience, knew the importance of warnings. How often he warns these people to be aware of the world, of the antichrists, these false teachers, and of false doctrines; to be aware of claiming great things in theory and forgetting to put them into practise. He warns them that it is useless to say you love God and yet to hate your brother; to give the impression of unusual devotion and yet not to be true in the ordinary details of your life.

John is full of warnings of that kind, and he actually ends this wonderful epistle, in which he has led us to the very highest heights of doctrine and of truth, on this note. Some might regard this as being methodical, but it is obviously not this, because John had a practical interest; there is nothing more dangerous than a theoretical interest in truth. John never wrote this letter merely to give a knowledge of truth as such; his object from the beginning was essentially practical—he wanted to help these people in their daily life and in their battle against the forces that are set against them in this world. So he is not concerned about stopping; he does not lead to a great oration and then suddenly stop. No; he is as practical as this: 'Little children, keep yourselves from idols'; that is his last word.

Now the way in which he uses this is of real interest. The great thing and the supreme thing is that we may know the only true and living God; that was the third of his great affirmations—'that we may know him that is true.' That is the thing that you must hold on to, says John, in spite of everything; the one thing that matters in this life and world is to know God. 'This is life eternal,' said our Lord himself, 'that they may know thee the only true God, and Jesus Christ, whom thou hast sent' (John 17:3). If we haven't that knowledge, says John, if we haven't that understanding, then we are not aware of the spiritual problems in which we are set, and we are obviously going to be defeated. And this knowledge of God is only to be obtained in Jesus Christ, who Himself is God; and if we know Him we have eternal life, as John has repeatedly reminded us.

So then, the vital thing is to know God, to walk with Him, and to abide in Him and in that knowledge. Nothing can ever go wrong with us if we are in that position, if we but walk in fellowship with God. That is what John is so anxious for these people to have–'that ye also may have fellowship with us: and truly our fellowship is with the Father, and with his Son Jesus Christ.'

'All right,' says John, 'that is the positive aspect of the truth. But if you want to make absolutely certain that you will be in that condition, keep yourselves from idols.' There are constantly things in this life and world that threaten to come between us and that knowledge of God. In other words, whether we like it or not, it is a warfare, it is a fight of faith; there is an enemy set against us. We have just been reminded of that–'that wicked one' that John speaks of towards the end of the letter; and the supreme object of that evil one is to come between us and this knowledge. And the way he does that, of course, is to try to get us to fix our mind and our attention and our heart upon something else. So it is in order to warn us against that terrible danger that John ends on this note.

Let me, therefore, put this in the form of three propositions. The first is that the greatest enemy that confronts us in the spiritual life is the worshipping of idols. The greatest danger confronting us all is not a matter of deeds or of actions, but of idolatry. That may sound strange to some. They may think that above all we need to be warned not to do certain things, and there are indeed great warnings like that in Scripture. But let us never forget that before we are told what not to do, we are always told what we *are* to do. Take the Ten Commandments–positive, then negative; they follow exactly the same procedure as John does here. Our deeds and actions are always the outcome of our attitudes and our thoughts. 'As a man thinks, so he is'; and if, therefore, you carefully scrutinize a man's

life, it is not at all difficult to discover what he really believes.
Actions are always the expression of a point of view, and that is why
the actions always proclaim the man. So the thing to concentrate
on is the outlook, the philosophy, the belief; and that is emphasised
everywhere in the Bible.

Now it was the cardinal error of the Pharisees that they were
so interested in the details of the 614 points of the law on which
they were so expert that they constantly forgot the great *principles*
of the law. They showed that on one occasion when they went to
our Lord and asked Him the question, 'Which is the first commandment of all?' They had been having a disputation amongst
themselves with regard to this matter, just as people still like to
argue whether one sin is greater than another. Our Lord replied,
'Thou shalt love the Lord thy God with all thy heart, and with all
thy soul, and with all thy mind, and with all thy strength: this is the
first commandment. And the second is like, namely this, Thou shalt
love thy neighbour as thyself' (Mark 12:30-31). That is the principle, for if that comes first, then our actions and our conduct and our
behaviour are likely to look after themselves. So the Scriptures
always start with this, and that is why the greatest danger in the
spiritual life, therefore, is always idolatry.

What does this mean? What is idolatry? Well, an idol can be
defined most simply in this way: an idol is anything in our lives that
occupies the place that should be occupied by God alone. Anything
that holds my life and my devotion, anything that is central in my
life, anything that seems to be vital, anything that is essential to me;
an idol is anything by which I live and on which I depend. Anything
that moves and rouses and attracts and stimulates me is an idol. An
idol is anything that I worship, anything to which I give much of
my time and attention, my energy and my money; anything that
holds a controlling position in my life is an idol.

Now when we look at it in that way, we see how practical this
advice of the Apostle is. The commentators have expended a good
deal of time and energy in dealing with the question of what John

IDOLATRY 197

meant when he said this. There are those who say this is perfectly simple. John was writing to people who had been pagan and who were still set in a pagan society, where idols had literally been made out of silver and gold and wood and stone and various other things, and he was just telling them not to go back and worship them. But surely that is an impossible suggestion; that was not the danger confronting these people. The danger was the teaching of the antichrists and the dangers that still confront Christian people always, everywhere. There is no suggestion in the New Testament that any of those people were liable to go back to literal idolatry in that sense.

The Protestant Fathers were, of course, very anxious to interpret these words in terms of the gross errors and the superstitions and the idolatry of Roman Catholicism, and of course an idol may indeed be an actual idol. But it does not stop at that; would to God it did! No; idolatry may consist of having false notions of God. If I am worshipping my own idea of God and not the true and living God, that is idolatry. That is something about which John is very concerned. These antichrists had been denying the teaching that Jesus Christ is come in the flesh. They had been denying that Jesus of Nazareth is the Son of God. And therefore, says John, if you claim that, and if your idea of God is not the biblical idea, if you have a false conception of Him and are worshipping such notions and conceptions, according to the Scripture that is simply idolatry.

So then, this may take the form of worshipping images and everything that is true of the Roman Catholic teaching—the worship of the Virgin Mary, the worship of the saints and praying to them; that is a form of idolatry. God alone is to be prayed to; God alone is to be worshipped—God the Father, God the Son, and God the Holy Spirit. He is the only true and living God—God in three Persons; no one else is to receive our devotion. That is the teaching of Scripture, and anyone to whom we give devotion beyond that makes us guilty of idolatry.

But let me go on to point out that idolatry can take many other forms. It is possible for us to worship our religion instead of wor-shipping God. How subtle a thing this idolatry is! We may think that we are worshipping God, but really we are simply worshipping our own religious observances and devotions. It is an error always of every Catholic type of religion that lays stress upon doing par-ticular things in particular ways, such as getting up and going to early-morning Communion. The emphasis may be more upon the observance of this rather than upon the worship of God.

I give that as but an illustration. It is not confined to the Catholic type; it is also found in the most evangelical circles. It is possible for us to worship not only our own religion but our own church, our own communion, our own religious body, our own particular community, our own particular sect, our own particular point of view—these are the things we may be worshipping. Theology has often become an idol to many people; they have really been worshipping ideas and not worshipping God. What a terrible thing this is; and yet, and I am sure we all must agree, how easy it is to forget the person of the Lord Jesus Christ and to stop at the ideas and the theories and the teaching concerning Him. How easy it is to stop, for instance, at the very doctrine of the Atonement and to forget the blessed person and what He suffered for me that I might be saved—and that is idolatry! Anything that occupies this central position rather than God Himself is idolatry. Also, there are people who worship their own experiences; they do not talk about God, they talk about themselves and what has hap-pened to them—always self in the foreground rather than God.

Further, the idol in the case of some people is their own coun-try; there are people who worship it. Are we guiltless of that? There are people who worship the state, or certain people in the state; there is a kind of mysticism that has often been developed. It was something of which the Stuart Kings became guilty, this almost deifying of the sovereign. And we have seen it in recent years in the dictatorships on the continent of Europe. But there are people still who worship the state—the power of the state and what the state can do for them; they live for it—it is their idol, their god.

But come, let us be still more careful in our self-examination—our idol may very well be another person. A man may make an idol of his wife; a wife may make an idol of her husband. Parents may really worship their children; the children may occupy in their minds and hearts the place that should be occupied by God. They give more time and attention and more thought to them; they are more concerned about them, and everything else, even attendance at church, may be put on one side because of the children. Any person that occupies in my life the place God should occupy I have turned into an idol; I have allowed that person to become an idol to me.

There are many people who worship their work, their profession. They live for it, they sacrifice all for it; God is pushed on one side in order that they might get on in their profession and their status. The position—this big thing, this thing they want above everything else, this thing for which they live—any such thing that occupies the place of God is idolatry. There is no difference in any sense between that and making a god out of gold or silver or wood or stone. You may say that is ridiculous, but it is the same thing. They did it with the hands, we do it in the spirit; and I am not sure but that our sin is worse than theirs.

But perhaps the supreme idol is self, for I suppose that in the last analysis we can trace all the others back to self. The people, for instance, who worship their country do so because it is *their* country. They do not worship another country, and that is for one reason only: they happen to have been born in this one rather than in that one. It is really themselves, and the same is true with children; it is because they are *your* children. And this other person? Well, it is the relationship in which that one person is something to *you*—it is always self. All the saints throughout the centuries have recognised this. The ultimate idol about which we have to be so careful is this horrible self—this concern about myself, putting myself where God ought to be. Everything revolving around *myself, my* interest, *my* position, *my* development, myself and all the things that result from that.

'Little children, keep yourselves from idols.' Beware that you do not put yourself in the place of God. The greatest danger in the spiritual life is idolatry, and it comes into all our activities. It comes into our Christian work; it is the greatest danger confronting a man standing in a pulpit preaching, a concern that he should preach in a particular manner. It comes into the activities we are engaged in. Let us examine ourselves as we think about these things. Idolatry— it is the greatest danger of all in the spiritual life.

So the second principle is that we must guard ourselves against this. 'Keep yourselves,' says John, which really means that we must guard ourselves as if we were in a garrison against this horrible danger of idolatry. Now you will notice that John tells us this is something that *we* have to do; it is not done for us. 'Keep yourselves from idols.' You do not 'Let go and let God.' No; you are always on guard— you watch and pray. You realise this terrible danger; *you* have to do it. At first sight John seems to be contradicting himself, because in the eighteenth verse he says, 'We know that whosoever is born of God sinneth not; but he that is begotten of God keepeth him, and that wicked one toucheth him not.' Oh, the comfort we derived as we considered that together; we know that everyone that is born of God does not go on sinning because He is kept by the Lord Jesus Christ. And yet here John is saying, 'Little children, *keep yourselves* from idols.' Is he contradicting himself? No; these things form the perfect balance that we always find in Scripture from beginning to end. It is simply John's way of saying, 'Work out your own salvation with fear and trembling: For it is God which worketh in you . . .' (Phil 2:12-13).

It is the same thing you find in the Old Testament, which says, 'Thou wilt keep him in perfect peace, whose mind is stayed on thee' (Isa 26:3). It does not stop at 'Thou wilt keep him in perfect peace'; He will do that, but only if the believer's mind is 'stayed' on Him. He will keep us, and the evil one will never get us back into his clutches; yes, that is true, but only if we keep ourselves from idols.

In other words, we must keep ourselves in right relationship to Him. If you and I keep our minds on the Lord Jesus Christ by the Holy Spirit, we need not worry. The Son of God will keep us, and the evil one will not be able to touch us. We do not have to meet the evil one in single combat; I am not fighting the devil directly, as it were. What I do is I keep myself in that right relationship with Christ, and He will defeat the enemy for me. I must be careful that some idol is not receiving my time and energy and the things that should be given to God. I must be constantly on the watch. I must beware, for there is an enemy with evil darts throwing these things at me. And realising all this, I must guard myself. I must guard my mind and understanding; I must watch my spirit and my heart. This is the most subtle thing in the world. It is the central temptation, so that I constantly have to watch and pray and ever and always be on my guard.

But that brings me to the last proposition, which is essentially practical. How is this to be done? How am I thus to guard myself from idols? It seems to me that the principles are quite simple.

The first thing we must always do is to remember the truth about ourselves. We must remember that we are God's people, that we are those whom Christ has purchased at the price and cost of His own precious blood. We must remember our destiny and the kind of life in which we are engaged and in which we walk. We must remember, as John has reminded us in the nineteenth verse, that 'We are of God, and the whole world lieth in the wicked one.' In other words, if we are of God and belong to God, then we must live for God, and we must not live for any of those other things. It does not matter what they are—I must not live for anything in this life and world. I can use them but not abuse them. God has given me these gifts; but if I turn any of them into my god, I am abusing them—I am worshipping the creature rather than the Creator. Oh, the tragedy that we should be doing that! The way to avoid that is to realise what I am; I am to exercise this 'understanding' that Christ has given me through the Holy Spirit, as we saw in verse 20.

I am to remember that I am not of this world, and therefore I must not live for or worship anything that belongs to it.

Or we can put that in the form of a second principle: I must remember the true nature of idols. That is the way to avoid worshipping them and a very good way of guarding yourself against idolatry. Just look and consider what they are, and there again is something we need to be reminded of constantly. Look at the things to which we tend to give our worship and our adoration; even if we put them at their highest and their best, are they worthy of it? Is there anything in this world of time which is worthy of our worship and our devotion? We know full well there is not. There is nothing in this world that lasts; everything is only temporary, everything is moving on to an end. There is nothing lasting and eternal; they are thus unworthy of our worship. They are all gifts given to us by God, so let us use them as such; let us not regard them as worthy of our entire devotion. Is it not tragic to think of a human soul worshipping money, possession, position, success, any person, children, or anything else of this life and world? It is all passing away. There is one alone who is worthy, and that is God.

And that is the last thing to remember. The way ultimately to keep ourselves from idols is to remember the truth about God and to live in communion with Him. Whenever we are tempted to engage in idolatry, let us think again of the nature and the being of God. Let us remember that the privilege that is offered to us is to worship Him and to walk with Him, to know Him and to commune and converse with Him, to be a child of God and to go on and spend eternity in His holy presence.

> *The dearest idol I have known,*
> *Whate'er that idol be,*
> *Help me to tear it from Thy throne,*
> *And worship only Thee.*

> William Cowper

How right he is! It is as we realise this wondrous possibility of knowing God that everything else should pale into insignificance. In other words, the Apostle's final advice, it seems to me, can be put like this: we must strive, without ceasing, to realise the presence and the fellowship and the communion of God. There was a prayer that Hudson Taylor, the great pioneer missionary to China, was very fond of, and we cannot do better than follow in the steps of that saintly, mighty man of God. After his death they found a sheet of paper in his diary on which he had written these words, and he obviously moved it from day to day as his diary went along. This, according to Hudson Taylor, was the most important thing in life for him:

> *Lord Jesus make thyself to me*
> *A living bright reality,*
> *More present to faith's vision keen,*
> *Than any outward object seen,*
> *More dear, more intimately nigh,*
> *Than e'en the sweetest earthly tie.*

That is it. To realise His nearness and His presence, to realise His companionship, to know that we are with Him and in Him, and to see to it always and ever that nothing and no one shall ever come between us and Him.

NOTES

CHAPTER 1: The New Testament Definition of a Christian
1. Cf. *The Love of God* (Crossway Books, 1994).

CHAPTER 2: The Wholeness of the Christian Life
1. For a further treatment of this, cf. *Fellowship with God* (Crossway Books, 1993).
2. See *The Love of God* (Crossway Books, 1994).
3. *Ibid.*
4. See *ibid.*

CHAPTER 5: How Faith Overcomes
1. This sermon was preached during the 1950 election campaign in Britain.
2. Cf. *Walking with God* (Crossway Books, 1993).

CHAPTER 10: The Life of God
1. The founder of the China Inland Mission, now the Overseas Missionary Fellowship.

CHAPTER 12: Prayer for the Brethren
1. See *Children of God* and *The Love of God* (Crossway Books, 1993 and 1994 respectively).

CHAPTER 13: Safe in the Arms of Jesus
1. Cf. *Children of God* (Crossway Books, 1993).

CHAPTER 14: The Life of the World
1. Cf. *Fellowship with God* (Crossway Books 1993).
2. Cf. *Walking with God* (Crossway Books, 1993).

CHAPTER 16: Understanding
1. This sermon was preached on Whit Sunday, 1950.

CHAPTER 17: Idolatry
1. The other sermons in this series are to be found in the first four volumes (*Fellowship with God, Walking with God, Children of God,* and *The Love of God,* published by Crossway Books).